EAST ANGLIAN
EX-LIBRIS

Peter Pears
&
Benjamin Britten

EAST ANGLIAN EX-LIBRIS

*Bookplates and labels made between
1700 and the present day*

John Blatchly

The Bookplate Society

2008

The Bookplate Society is an international society of collectors, bibliophiles, artists and others dedicated to promoting bookplate use and study.

Each year the Society publishes two issues of *Bookplate Journal* (ISSN 0264-3693) and *The Bookplate Society Newsletter* (ISSN 0309-7935).

Every two years, members receive a book on the work of a particular artist, or a specific theme, sometimes topographical. For details of books in print, forthcoming publications and membership benefits see the Society's website: www.bookplatesociety.org.

Our email addresses are: publications@bookplatesociety.org and members@bookplatesociety.org

© 2008 John Blatchly

400 copies of which 150 are for sale

ISBN 978-0-9555428-1-7

This sequel to *Some Norfolk and Suffolk Ex-Libris*, 2000 (ISBN 0-9535008-3-3) is published by The Bookplate Society, Yarkhill, Upper Bucklebury, Reading, Berks. RG7 6QH

Design and formatting by James Shurmer

Printed by Henry Ling Ltd., Dorchester DT1 1HD

Front cover: Jacobean armorial for Sir Thomas Hare Baronet, 1734 (page 35)

Back cover: Pictorial for William H. Booth by Robert Anning Bell, 1896 (page 9)

Frontispiece: Pictorial label for Peter Pears and Benjamin Britten by Reynolds Stone, 1970 (page 113)

Title page: Rebus plate wood-engraved for the author by John Craig, 2007 (page 120)

Tailpiece: Tradecard or bookplate of William Brown of Ipswich (1778–1851), Greek Revival architect and timber merchant (page 128)

Contents

Preface

MANY YEARS AGO, stimulated by discovering the W.H. Booth Collection of Suffolk Bookplates in the Suffolk Record Office (S097), I set about collecting originals or good images of a very large number of East Anglian ex-libris. A first selection of these was illustrated and discussed in *Some Suffolk and Norfolk Ex-libris* published by the Bookplate Society as the members' book for the millennium year (*SNXL* from here on). Some two hundred extra copies were made available within the two counties, of which a few remain to be offered with this sequel to those who failed to secure the first volume. The two books belong together, because insights developed while compiling the first have led to the discovery of more plates by some of the engravers and designers featured, as references to *SNXL* show in what follows. An account of the interesting and sometimes distinguished ex-libris used by W.H. Booth himself is given first.

Through the courtesy of Lord De Saumarez, then owner of Shrubland Hall, in *SNXL* I was able to survey the ex-libris in books in his library. Books originally belonging to almost a dozen families came together there as the result of as many intermarriages. Sadly, none of those books remain at Shrubland today, so that account was timely in preserving a record of what had been there.

The present volume has an account of the ways in which another family collected books over four centuries, marking their ownership in interesting and unusual ways. I am most grateful to Lord Tollemache for his kindness in allowing me to study his extensive library in depth during monthly visits to the moated Tudor Helmingham Hall and to publish my findings. He is kind enough to call me his honorary librarian, but that implies work rather than the great pleasure which comes of making regular discoveries.

If any century is neglected compared with the first book it is the nineteenth, but a substantial label section makes up for that. I hope that it will also be some compensation to have a varied survey of East Anglian ex-libris made since 1900, including some made by highly gifted but little known figures, and others by artists and engravers at work today.

I make no apology for being even readier than I was before to attribute plates to their artists. It is partly experience, but also the feeling that it is often possible to suggest who was available to make a particular bookplate or label. Suggestions are no more than that, and readers are invited to come up with other ideas for consideration.

Once more I must pay tribute to the excellent grounding in the study of ex-libris which I received over about twenty years from my good friend the late Brian North Lee. It may be that the lack of his wisely restraining hand has rendered me less cautious, but every pupil has eventually to do without the teacher, and he was still helping me greatly in the early stages of compiling this book. Dr John Pickles FSA of Cambridge has been an invaluable source of information about that town and county; to them both I am grateful indeed.

JOHN BLATCHLY

Graphic sources and acknowledgements

The majority of the illustrations are taken from original bookplates and labels in the author's collection. A few bookplates from the Booth Collection are reproduced by permission of the Suffolk Record Office, and the rare Hargrave label comes from the Stuart Johnson collection at Kensington Public Library. Thanks to permission from the executors, bookplates in the collection of the late John Simpson were scanned prior to their sale at Bonham's in May 2005, and several images come from that source. Anthony Pincott has kindly allowed me to illustrate ex-libris from his collection, and has given generously of his time to turn most of the illustrations into a digital format. The Charles Hall Crouch Collection at the Society of Antiquaries of London, and the Franks, Viner, Banks and Ambrose Heal collection at the British Museum have provided others. Special thanks are due to Paul Latcham for his photography in the Department of Prints and Drawings there, and to James Shurmer for taking pride in designing this book. Geoffrey Vevers kindly read the whole final draft and detected several errors; any that remain can only be mine. Ron Fiske's incomparable collection for Norfolk has been drawn upon once again, as have the vast resources of Jim Wilson.

Abbreviations

SNXL	*Some Suffolk and Norfolk Ex-libris,* John Blatchly, (Bookplate Society, 2000)
F	Number in Gambier Howe's *Catalogue of the Franks Collection of British and American Bookplates*, (British Museum 1903–04)
NIF	Not in the Franks Collection
V	Number in the Viner Collection
ODNB	*Oxford Dictionary of National Biography*, (Oxford 2003)
BJ	*The Bookplate Journal*: First series 1983–2002; Second series 2003–
IGI	International Genealogical Index
British BP	*British Bookplates*, Brian North Lee, (Newton Abbot 1979)
Fincham	*The Artists and Engravers of British and American Bookplates*, H.W. Fincham (London 1897)

Catherine, wife of Lionel Tollemache, later 1st baronet, holding a carnation and aged 35 in 1599. Attributed to Robert Peake the elder

Lionel Tollemache, baron Huntingtower and 4th earl Dysart, aged 19 in 1727, the year he succeeded his grandfather. Painted in Venice by Rosalba Carriera

Almanacks for the years 1743 to 1746 bound in elaborately gilt-stamped morocco, the arms of Tollemache at the foot of each spine.

PLATE I

Three gilt-stamped superlibros used by the fourth earl Dysart

(*Top left*) Arms and crest of Tollemache

(*Top right*) Arms at foot of shield and crest, with LHTD monogram

(*Below*) Earl's coronet above double ED cypher for Earl Dysart between feathered plumes

PLATE II

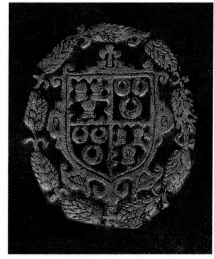

(*Above*) Gilt superlibros of Sir Robert Kemp used in 1631

(*Left*) Upper board of Bible (Paris 1605) belonging to Henry Prince of Wales. The letters HP for Henricus Princeps on either side of the Royal arms and decorative corner devices are all gilt stamped. Original (4½ inches wide)

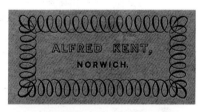

Four labels on coloured paper:
George Burrell of Thetford
Henry Leach of Wisbech
Alfred Kent of Norwich
Frederick Durham of Stratford St Andrew

PLATE III

(*Above*) Pictorial for A.N.L. 'Tim' Munby

(*Left*) Hand coloured and inscribed:
Jacobean armorial of Beaupré Bell
(*reduced in size*)

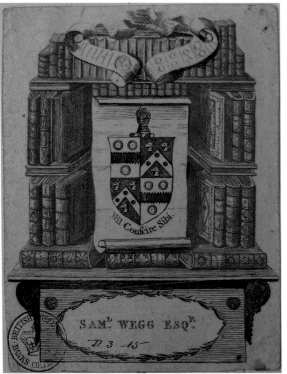

Two plates in which the plate was differentially
inked in colours:

(*Above*) Crest plate for John Benjafield of
Dorset. Printed in two colours

(*Left*) Bookpile spade shield armorial for
Samuel Wegg Esqr

PLATE IV

William Henry Booth: the ex-libris of a collector

According to W.T. Pike in his *Norfolk and Suffolk Contemporary Biographies* (Brighton 1911) William Henry Booth of Ipswich, coal factor, was a 'collector of antiquities, lover of the fine arts and literature' and owned 'a very fine collection of old English and American bookplates, particularly of the Chippendale period'.

Of that collection only the Suffolk section remains, though occasionally small numbers of his bookplates surface, mounted on pale blue thin card, the surface usually flecked with tiny fibres. As recently as 1992 Thomas Thorp of Guildford offered the author a dozen or so of Booth's plates, his hand unmistakeable. Some 250 Suffolk plates and labels, mounted in the same characteristic way with biographical details, notes on provenance, related ephemera and prices paid by Booth (in his own code), can be seen at the Suffolk Record Office in Ipswich (S097). It is not known how they came there.

In the collection there are copies of his personal bookplates, including correspondence with makers and even invoices. Booth was a member of the Ex Libris Society from 1897 to 1908, then of the Bookplate Exchange Club until his death in 1928. The rarity of many plates in this small but extremely interesting collection was one spur to writing the present book and its predecessor.

Born in 1861, Booth was educated at Cheltenham College, and in about 1885 took over the family business from his father David Henry Booth, JP and mayor of Ipswich in 1880 (who used

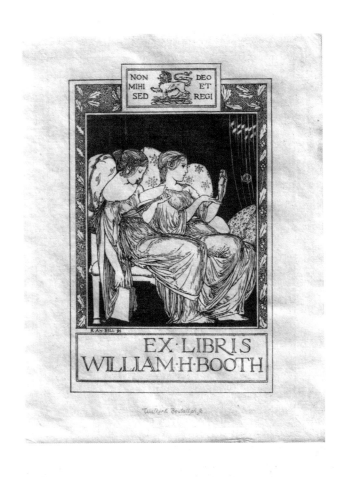

NON MIHI SED | DEO ET REGI

EX·LIBRIS WILLIAM·H·BOOTH

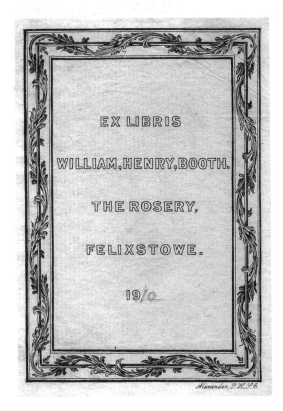

EX LIBRIS

WILLIAM, HENRY, BOOTH.

THE ROSERY,

FELIXSTOWE.

19 1 0

·EX·LIBRIS·

·WM·H·BOOTH

a modest printed label at Pembridge House in Anglesea Road). William Booth often moved house, a difficult thing for one who collected furniture, books, silver, Lowestoft porcelain and paintings. At each move he commissioned a new ex-libris; for Alandale in 1892 he had a diamond-shaped engraved label (see previous page), but the designer and the cost are unknown.

The next move was to his grandest residence, Handford Lodge, the house enlarged from that of Samuel Kilderbee, town clerk in the 18th century, by Peter Schuyler Bruff, CE, who brought the Eastern Union Railway to Ipswich in 1846. Here Booth commissioned his finest plate from Robert Anning Bell. It is a pictorial signed and dated 1896, printed by Walker & Boutall of Clifford's Inn, Fleet Street. This was Anning Bell's first ex-libris to be printed from a photo intaglio plate, and Booth ordered it in two sizes, 123 by 181 mm and 85 by 112 mm, the former in black and in three other shades – orange, red and red-brown. The printing bill came to £11 10s, but Bell's design fee is not disclosed.

Under 'Recent Bookplates' in the *Ex Libris Journal* (Vol. 7, 1897, 157) the plate is described as 'very effective', 'the pose of the figures… decidedly graceful'. One girl is holding a Egyptian statuette, no doubt one of Booth's treasures. 'We believe that Mr Booth is averse to exchanging this plate, except for something exceptionally good.' In 1906, most of the contents of Handford Lodge were sold, then the house itself. What occasioned this upheaval is not known.

The sale catalogue cover (by the artist and architect John Shewell Corder) is decorated with several of Booth's prize possessions, his Anning Bell bookplate amongst them. Although a library of 3,000 volumes was sold, there were no bookplate lots, so Booth took his ex-libris to Felixstowe.

Here for The Rosery, Booth commissioned two ex-libris: first in 1910 a label from A. Alexander of Westmoreland Place, City Road, Etching and Art Printer, who added 'old-style open lettering' to a older copper bearing only a foliage trail border. Booth had bought this together with coppers for the plates in John Gage's two great works: *History of Hengrave* and *History of Thingoe Hundred* at the sale of Hengrave Hall in 1897. Alexander's bill, including 250 book labels (100 by 127 mm) on Superior Antique paper, was £1 4s 7d; half the plates were given an added buff tint.

By 1914 Booth found a local designer for a new pictorial showing him in his library and, through an open window, the Cork lightship. Philip J. Thornhill of Langer Ridge, Felixstowe was the artist and W.S. Cowell Ltd of Ipswich used a zinc plate to produce 250 ordinary and a few large-paper copies for a total of 13s 6d. For a second impression in 1922 the letters CORK on the side of the ship were blocked out.

Philip H. Ottaway was the artist of the last of Booth's plates, a pictorial showing the garden of Booth's next house, Chiltern in Henley Road, Ipswich. The design cost four guineas, but Cowells charged only 18s to make the block and print the plates. The stone heron is no longer at Chiltern, but has crossed the road where it thrives in another garden. Of William Booth's early homes, only Alandale, The Rosery and Chiltern have escaped demolition. His last move was to a house in Park Road which survives but for which no special ex-libris was devised.

Ex-libris Helminghamae

No family but Tollemache has ever occupied the moated Tudor Hall at Helmingham in Suffolk, and there is no other house in the kingdom where the drawbridge is still raised nightly. John Tollemache of Bentley Hall had by 1492 bought the lordship of Helmingham, and his eldest son Lionel, the first of seven of that name, married Edith, daughter and heiress of Edmund Joyce of that parish, thus acquiring the estates to surround the house which he built early in the sixteenth century.

Two members of the family stand out as builders of the house's library: the first Catherine, who in 1575 married the fourth Lionel, 1st Baronet and Knight of the Bath. She was daughter of Henry, 2nd Lord Cromwell of Elmham in Norfolk, a woman of great spirit and wide accomplishments. The books she collected showed her strong interests in housekeeping, medicine and Protestant theology. She was a competent herald, designing and probably painting herself a family tree divided horizontally on the walls of two bedchambers and, when widowed, she blessed her eldest son's marriage with painted arms of the match in the spandrels of the fireplace arch in the great chamber.

It would have been truly remarkably if Catherine had adopted any form of ex-libris other than the characteristic ownership inscription she applied to some of her books and manuscripts. 'Catheren Tallemache ow[n]eth this boocke' marks her MS Book of Secrets of which the present 5th Baron Tollemache presented a scholarly edition with facsimiles (including her own Receipts of Pastrey, etc) to his fellow members of the Roxburghe Club in 2001. Catherine's copy of *The Substanec* [sic] *of Christian Religion*, by Amandus Polanus, (London 1600) (shelfmark LK 2.15) has the same inscription with the omission of the final e of the surname. Her portrait from the Hall is in Plate I.

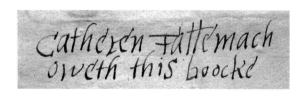

The Eighteenth Century

Lionel Tollemache, Baron Huntingtower and 5th baronet, became 4th earl of Dysart on the death of his grandfather in 1727 and enjoyed the estates at Helmingham, Ham, Woodhey, Bawdsey and Brantham until his death in 1770. Lionel Wilbraham his father had died in 1712 aged thirty, and owned a New Testament copiously illustrated with woodcuts and sold by Thomas Guy in London in 1687 (LF 2.3). Labelled in manuscript by its first owner, it was brought from Woodhey in October 1741 and given by the fourth Earl to his second son Wilbraham.

For forty-three years the fourth Earl gave free rein to his love of books and reading. Despite a reputation for economy he sat for three portraits in Venice in 1727 and 1728, the first in pastel

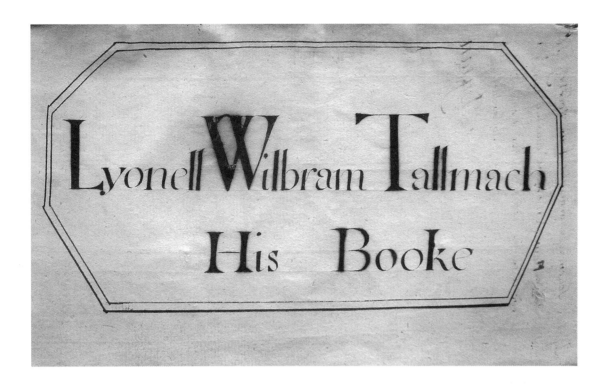

by the artist most celebrated in that medium, Rosalba Carriera, the other two, with and without armour, by Boreola Nazari. He was also an avid collector of books, frequenting the bookshops of Venice, Milan and Amsterdam, and a voracious reader. He recorded on fly-leaves where he bought and where he read them 'perlegi apud...', with notes, often extensive, of the principal matters he wished to remember. In a copy of Martialis, *Epigrammata in usum Scholae Westmonasteriensis*, 1721 (LDR B3.6), he wrote 'The gift of Mr Thomas Fitzgerald, usher of the Third Form when I was at Westminster School, for which I made him a present of Five Guineas', both gift and purchase it seems.

One particularly moving survival in the library is *La Bible* printed in Geneva in 1605 by Matthieu Berjon (LF 2.8) which had belonged to Prince Henry, elder brother of the future Charles I. To explain its presence it must be explained that the Dysart earldom had descended to the family *via* the female line, the first Earl, Will Murray, having been ennobled by Charles I to compensate him for the humiliation he had suffered as his surrogate whipping boy. After Henry's death of typhoid fever, aged 18, in 1612, Prince Charles probably gave the book to his friend and companion Murray, and so it came eventually to Helmingham. The initials H and P for Henricus Princeps surround the royal arms all gilt-stamped on front and back boards. it has remains of green silk ties rather than clasps.

Lionel Tollemache, baron Huntingtower and 4th earl of Dysart used to experiment with his four initials in search of the ideal monogram for the endpapers of his books. LTHD is the most logical and commonest arrangement, but LHDT, LTHD and LDHT can all be found – even DHTL. When it came to ex-libris, the earl planned the most elaborate suite of devices for gilt-stamping the boards and spines of his books which this writer has ever encountered. There were also two armorial bookplates, one small and anonymous, the other for Lionel Talmash, Earl of Dysart and signed by John Clark, engraver and print seller of Gray's Inn. The Tollemache arms are Argent a fret Sable, and the motto 'Confido conquiesco' means 'I trust and

Lionel Talmash

Earl of Dyfart.

John Clark
Engraver
and Print-Seller,
in Grays Inn
LONDON.

VIVE LE BURIN.

Where may be had all sorts of Maps or Prints, & great variety of Books for Youth to Draw after. The best black-Lead Pencils; Right Indian-Ink, & Water-Colours . At which Place are Engrav'd Steel or Silver-Seals & Stamps, Names cut on Brass or Wood for the Use of such as cannot Write . Also Arms, Crests & Cyphers on Gold & Silver Plate: Copper-Plates for Books & other Uses; Blank Notes for Bankers, Shop-keepers-Bills &c. At Reasonable Rates.

am content'. It is quite likely that Clark supplied (or arranged the supply of) the tools for the gilt stamping, but that may never be confirmed. Clark's elegant tradecard shows that he enjoyed grand gestures.

One of the superlibros on the Dysart books appeared to earlier writers as the monogram CB in ligature under an earl's coronet, which they could not explain. Their CB is in fact ED which makes immediate sense. Another eccentric design consists of an LHT monogram with the final D closed by means of part of a crescent, yet another of the earl's experiments with initials.

The date of the main campaign to improve the appearance and durability of the earl's better books seems to have been 1737 as the frequent inscription 'among the old books at Helmingham new bound in 1737' shows. In 1741 Woodhey in Cheshire was found too damp for the family, never mind the books, and that October the library was transported to Helmingham. Many of Dysart's lesser books remain in quarter calf and colourful Italian block printed paper boards. At this time he was a subscriber for Thomas Osborne's trade catalogues and bought judiciously from them, perhaps with the advice of the Joseph Brereton, son of third earl's steward. Brereton (1721–87), a considerable collector himself, was educated at Queens' College, Cambridge, as his earlier booklabels, probably printed at Bury St Edmunds, show (one is F3624). The third (NIF) links him firmly to Helmingham, and from his graduation as LL.B and ordination in 1744 and his presentation to the Dysart living of Acton in Cheshire the following year, he probably acted as chaplain to the family and librarian to its head. His manuscript catalogue of the library up to 1762 remains at Helmingham (T/Hel/9/2/1).

Later bookplates and labels (none in Franks)

The Dysart line moved away from Helmingham after the death in 1840 aged 95 of Louisa, the almost blind 7th Countess of Dysart. Her sister Jane had married John Delap Halliday, and their son Admiral John Halliday (1772–1837) assumed the name of Tollemache in 1821. It was his son John who was created 1st Baron Tollemache in 1876. Early in the nineteenth century the admiral used a simple spade shield armorial with crest, and sometime after 1876 the new peer went to Allan Wyon for a Tollemache armorial with coronet and supporters as was now correct. Wilbraham Frederick, his son, succeeded him in 1890. He died in 1904 and his second wife Mary Stuart, daughter of Lord Claude Hamilton, survived him, living at Helmingham until her death in 1939 with the Hall gently crumbling around her. To protect the books, pictures and furnishings from the adverse effects of sunlight, all the windows were painted green, and when it rained she found an umbrella useful, even in bed.

TOLLEMACHE.

1900.

Mary Tollemache

M. S. T.

Helmingham Hall

The dowager Lady Tollemache continued to patronise the Wyons, commissioning an armorial, dated 1900, rather late in her husband's life and, for herself after his death, three ex-libris: an armorial with Tollemache impaling Hamilton, a label for Mary Tollemache with coronet and border printed in brown and a small one with just M.S.T. in sans serif type. His armorial and her brown label are both signed by Wyon. Copies of her armorial are still wrapped in the green paper they were posted in, on the white printed label: 'Allan Wyon, artist and engraver to His Majesty the King' and a crowned E.R.I.

From Thomas Moring 'Atte Ye GRIFFINS' 44 High Holborn 'Heraldic Engraver who has ye Prize medal', came a fine brass library stamp which has to be pressed into a pad charged with something akin to printer's ink. It is very hard to obtain a perfect impression, and anything less is defacing to books which deserve better. The label in the lid of the box was badly defaced by the same ink, but most could be removed with white spirit and a soft cloth.

Eighteenth- and Nineteenth-Century ex-libris

The Kemp family of Gissing

This large armorial with tassels between the mantling and the motto scroll characteristic of early designs (F16946) must be for Robert Kemp (1667–1734) before he succeeded his father as 3rd Bart in 1710. His choice of motto, reflecting the three garbs (sheaves of wheat), comes from Psalm 126: 'Qui seminant in lachrymis in exultatione metent'; 'Who sow in tears shall reap in joy'. The engrailed bordure is correctly or, but the field should be hatched for gules.

A much earlier Kemp mark of ownership is the gilt superlibros (in Ron Fiske's ownership, NIF, see Plate III) stamped on the boards of a second edition (1631) of John Selden's *Titles of Honour* for which Sir Robert Kemp paid fifteen shillings in 1633. Then a knight, he was later created a baronet as a gentleman of the Privy Chamber to Charles I and made the king's will in

Sir William Kemp, Bar.t

1647. The quartering with Kemp is an ancient one, for any marriage with a Buttevelyn heiress took place in the early fourteenth century. As well as writing his name and the price on the titlepage, Sir Robert added the telling epigram 'parvis negate gloria magnus quies' which means 'the glory denied to small people is peace of mind'.

When the tenth baronet Sir William ordered an armorial (F16945) from Hewitt of Pickett Street before his ordination in 1811 he used the motto 'Lucem spero' first adopted by the Elizabethan Kemps; 'I hope for light'. He died in 1874 having served the parish of Gissing, near Diss in Norfolk, as rector for 58 years.

The Jerningham family of Costessey

Ever since Sir Henry Jernegan of Huntingfield in Suffolk showed himself Mary Tudor's first and most loyal supporter at Kenninghall during Lady Jane Grey's nine-day reign, the family has supported the old religion. It was his son Henry who changed the family name to Jerningham, and grandson Henry was created 1st Bart in 1621. From the 3rd Bart onwards the family adopted ex-libris, mostly armorial, the first example of which was made at Douai where the young Jerninghams were sent to the English College.

Sir Francis, born about 1650, succeeded his father in 1680 and died in 1730. It was in about 1710 that Vacheron made and signed his armorial with its long Latin inscription on a scroll (F16442). There are tassels, but not of the English type, and the oddest thing is the placing of the baronet's badge, not so much a red hand of Ulster but blood-spattered, in sinister base. The copper must have survived, for good nineteenth century impressions are not uncommon.

Sir John, son and heir of Francis, succeeded but died without heirs in 1737 when his brother Sir George became 5th Bart. He married Mary Plowden in 1733, and his early armorial has strange errors in the impaled coat (F16447). The motto (Virtue is the basis of life) belonged to the

Sr George   *Jerningham*

21

Stafford family with whom the Jerninghams were connected by marriage and for whom Vacheron also made a plate. A second armorial, a competent Jacobean properly titled (NIF, previous page below), must have lasted him until his death in 1774, aged 94.

It would require a longish article to do justice to all the Jerningham ex-libris; for example the next baronet Sir William had his plate (F16450) reworked six times. Three labels follow: theengraved one William used in his father's lifetime (NIF) and two neat typographic labels (one is F16445 above and NIF below) for Edward, poet and dramatist, third son of Sir George (1737–1812) and the only *ODNB* Jerningham after the first Sir Henry.

Freke of West Bilney

It is not certain whether this splendid early armorial (F11364), particularly its engraving, can be claimed for Norfolk. Percy Freke or Freake of Rathbury, later Castle Freke, Sheriff of Cork in 1694 and MP, came into the West Bilney estate near King's Lynn. His wife and kinswoman Elizabeth Freke bore him a son Percy who was MP for Bultimore and created a baronet in 1713; he died unmarried in Dublin in 1728. This was clearly his plate, of which late pulls exist in pale imitation of this sparkling impression. His brother Sir John Redmond Freke succeeded him but the baronetcy became extinct at his death in 1764.

The Folkes of Rushbrooke and Barton Magna

Silence Hanson became the second wife of the lawyer Thomas Folkes, third son of Martin and Elizabeth Folkes of Rushbrooke, in about 1690 and bore him five children between 1692 and 1709, of whom only Elizabeth survived to marry Sir Thomas Hanmer as his second wife. This dignified tasselled early armorial (F10856 overleaf), is no lady's plate and was surely engraved for Thomas soon after the marriage and renamed for his widow after his death and burial at Great Barton in 1730. If so, she had five years to use it before her death in January 1735. There is no record of Thomas's original plate.

Thomas' younger brother Martin was a bencher of Gray's Inn and father and namesake of a celebrated president of both Royal and Antiquarian Societies. This was Martin Folkes (*ODNB*,

Silence Folkes.

Engraved for the Universal Magazine.

Martin Folkes Esq.
Late President of the Royal Society.

For J. Hinton at the King's Arms in Newgate Street

Martin Folkes

1690–1754) whose early armorial (F10853) quartered Folkes and Lovell. His mother Dorothy was daughter and coheiress of William Lovell of Hillingdon Hall, Norfolk, where she and her husband retired and died. We may certainly claim the famous Martin Folkes as East Anglian.

The Edgar family of Ipswich

Thomas Edgar, Recorder of Ipswich and his wife Mary Powle of Grimstone House, Ipswich had two sons, Thomas (1646–77) and Devereux (1651–1739). Although Thomas junior left an heir Mileson and had the Red House built for him by his father about a mile northeast, when the recorder died Devereux Edgar seems to have assumed the headship of the family. He married Temperance, daughter of Robert Sparrow of Wickhambrook and became a prominent and energetic figure in the town: Tory politician, churchman, magistrate, major in the Militia, diarist of political events and much more. The Whigs were unwise to oust him and four like-minded colleagues from the bench in 1709, for when Queen Anne heard of it she commanded that three of them be reinstated, to general popular rejoicing.

The five known Edgar ex-libris are quite hard to assign to owners, but there is no doubt that the first (F9542) has the correct cadency mark for Devereux though it is hard to date the composition which was re-engraved twice, once for his eldest son and heir Robert (1682–1750; F9547) who came of age in 1703. One dares to suggest more of Hillyard's work here. Robert's first cousin Mileson's plate (1677–1713; F9546) lacks a helm but the crest rests on something resembling a bell. The crest for M: Edgar (NIF) would fit another Mileson (1730–1804) and the Col. Mileson (1760–1830) who mutilated a Robert plate in 1784 married Robert's grand-daughter Susanna Edgar (which might explain how he obtained it). The elegant engraved calligraphic frame with 'Miss M. Edgar 25th Octr 1836' in manuscript illustrated in *BJ*, 4, 100 is likely to be for a Mary of this family.

Robert Hamby of Ipswich

Robert Hamby (1710–74) was, like his father Robert, an attorney of St Mary at the Elms parish. He wrote his name in red ink in the blank scroll of unusual design beneath the achievement on the bookplate, until his father died in 1735 'Ro: Hamby Iuns.,' and plain 'Ro: Hamby' thereafter. He married Elizabeth Mary Roberts in 1742. Their impressive urn memorial and hatchments are in the Elms church. There has been much confusion over his date of death and place of burial, but although registers throw no light on the latter, his will was proved in the Prerogative Court of Canterbury in October 1774. It has just been realised that a portrait by Gainsborough for long labelled Robert Hornby Esq, painted in about 1752, is in fact Hamby's. That year, the painter brought his family to Ipswich, and will have needed a lawyer's services when taking a suitable house in Lower Brook Street. Perhaps he paid his fees in kind.

The Petres of Writtle, Thorndon and Ingatestone

As the model for the baron hero of Alexander Pope's *Rape of the Lock*, Robert, 7th Lord Petre, had a suitably imposing armorial bookplate (F23403). It was at Binfield in 1711 that Lord Robert playfully cut a lock from the head of the beautiful Arabella Fermor whom he had been courting. His action and Pope's mock-epic poem both gave the Fermor family offence and it is unsurprising that the match was called off. In any case, Robert died of smallpox the next year, aged only 24. Pope had to print an explanation in later editions that his heroine Belinda was *not* Arabella.

Robert was succeeded by his yet unborn son Robert James, who became a distinguished botanist, elected FRS at 18, and is remembered in the botanical genus *Petrea*. He married Anne, daughter of James, 3rd earl of Derwentwater in 1732 and died in 1742; their arms are impaled in the Jacobean armorial F23406. Robert James the scholar is likely to have added largely to the Petre library.

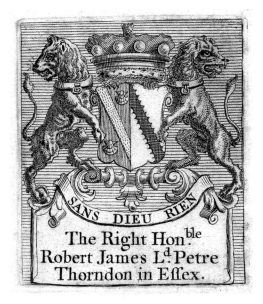

SANS DIEU RIEN

The Right Honble
Robert James Ld Petre
Thorndon in Essex.

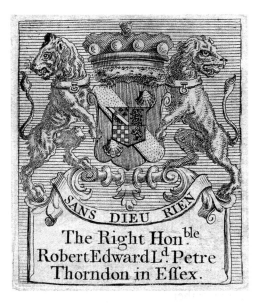

SANS DIEU RIEN

The Right Honble
Robert Edward Ld Petre
Thorndon in Essex.

William Bernard Lord Petre.

William Petre

Engraved by Valenti Romei

The Hon.ble Edward Petre.

His son Robert Edward, 9th baron, had his father's plate reworked with Howard in pretence for his first wife Anne, daughter of Philip Howard of Buckenham, Norfolk (F23404). In 1788 he married another Howard, Juliana, daughter of Henry Howard of Glossop, and then used a spade shield armorial with Howard shown twice, in pretence and impaled (F23405). The modest diesinker for the Hon. Edward, a son of the second marriage, with Petre quartering Walmesley (the Derwentwater name) is F23408. His horses won the St Leger three years running from 1827.

The next baron to have a bookplate was the 12th, William Bernard, who succeeded in 1850. His and his wife's Clifford arms are impaled in a modern Jacobean design (F23407).

Monsignor William Petre, subsequently 13th baron, and founder of the Petre library at Downside, ordered his armorial from Valenti while on some embassy in Rome (F23410). There is some uncertainty about who disposed of the family's collection, not a large one, but with at least two Caxtons. It may have been the 12th baron wishing to build newly-permitted Catholic churches in Essex, or the 13th to finance the school for Catholic gentry he had founded. A fine Book of Hours surfaced again when the Foyle library at Beeleigh Abbey was sold.

The present 18th Baron Petre, Essex's Lord Lieutenant, helped greatly with this summary.

Precursors of the Swaffham Jacobeans

In *SNXL*, pages 37–41, all the known Jacobean and Chippendale armorials of two closely related stock patterns were illustrated with the suggestion that they were made in the 1730s by Thomas Gardiner, bell founder of Swaffham. No further examples have come to light since then. There were three varieties of the schoolmaster Charles Squire's plate with the same arms as a cruder Jacobean dated 1716 for Thomas Squire (F27799), perhaps Charles' father. Three characteristics: titling, mantling style and shield shape have been used to assemble a small group of similar armorials earlier than the 'Gardiner' group by as much as twenty years.

1 THO=SQUIRE=MDCCXVI (F27799)

2 Robert Crow SWAFFHAM (F7480; the coat is for Crow of East Bilney)

3 G. Langdale (F17565), probably Godfrey of Huntingdon, born at Longthorpe, Yorks in 1674 and died in Huntingdon on new year's day, 1737. He married Margaret Sayer of Huntingdon in about 1702, but his plate has only single arms.

4 Robert Izard, Royston (F16145) married Grace Cox in 1718 and their arms are impaled.

THO: SQUIRE: MDCCXVI

Robert Crow
SWAFFHAM.

Henricus Crofs-grove Norvici.
Typographus Natus Aug. 14. 1683.

Langdale

5 Henry Cross-grove, Norwici Typographus Natus Aug. 19 1686 (F7462). His *ODNB* entry contradicts the inscription on the bookplate, which should read 'Natus Aug. 14 1683'; he died in 1744. A colourful character of Irish extraction who was Jacobite, journalist and printer, he was the proprietor of the *Norwich Gazette* (See *ODNB*). The armorial certainly belongs to the group, but both known copies are badly mutilated (the other in Coll. J.L. Wilson) and seems originally to have been intended for one of the many Huguenot families in Norwich. Henry Crossgrove must have known whose arms they were (could it be for Samuel Hasbart, a Norwich distiller of uncertain origin who until 1718 was Henry's partner?). Cross-Grove perhaps employed the designer and engraver of this group.

Robert Izard Royston

EXALTAVIT HUMILES

Sr. Lister Holte of Aston in Warwick Shire Bar.nt

THEREUPON

Fr: Masson Rector of Shotesham

6 Sr. Lister Holte of Aston in Warwick Shire Barnt. (F15185), who succeeded his father Charles in 1729 and died in 1769. Franks noted, without giving a location for the earlier state, that Lister's was reworked from Charles' plate. Although the Holtes were of Warks, the inscription and the mantling strongly resemble others in this group.

Francis Masson of Shottisham

FRANCIS MASSON was instituted to the vicarage of Shottisham All Saints a few miles south of Norwich on 6 November 1718. When designing his own punning and bogus heraldic Jacobean armorial he adopted a baronet's helm (NIF). The shield is divided per fess azure and sable (sky and earth?) and there are two gold mason's trowels and a triangular foundation stone laid on the ground. The perspective is hopeless, but the motto 'Thereupon' gives the first clue. To make things plainer, Masson inserted his text on the empty ends of the motto scroll: 'I. Cor'. 'III. X':

> According to the grace of God which is given unto me, as a wise master builder, I have laid the foundation and another buildeth thereon. But let every man take heed how he buildeth thereupon.

Two large early Norwich labels

PECKOVER OF FAKENHAM. The printed label dated 1721 for JOSEPH PECKOVER of Fakenham shares a bold decorative device with the undated label for the Hargraves of Norwich. It is likely that both were the work of either Henry Cross-Grove or William Chase, the two most active printers in the city at the time. Edmund and Mary Peckover christened a son Joseph in 1658 who would have been 63 in 1721. It is therefore better to look to the next generation, and the Joseph already mentioned and wife Catherine had nine sons and five

daughters between 1687 and 1704. They christened three of the sons to be their father's namesake, but the first two (born 1689 and 1691) died in infancy. Only Joseph, born 1697, survived, and he would have been 24 when the label was printed, just the age to be buying a printed keep-sake at Norwich. He married Anne Wright at Tasburgh, Norfolk, in 1728 bringing her back to Fakenham where she died in 1744.

HARGRAVE of NORWICH. Hannah Borage married Isaac Walsingham, probably of Smallburgh, as his second wife, in 1701. They christened two children at Bradfield Independent Chapel: Ursula in 1703 and Edward in 1705. Between then and 1711 Isaac died leaving Hannah free to marry 39-year-old BENJAMIN HARGRAVE at St Helen's, Norwich, who obviously preferred to call her Jo[-]hannah. The three children of their marriage, Samuel, Johannah and Josiah were christened at the Octagon Chapel between 1713 and 1718, but it appears that none of them survived their mother, who died, twice widowed, in 1743. Her will leaves everything to

(98%)

'my only children' of her first marriage. By now both of them had married: Edward to Mary Ives at St Michael Coslany in 1723 and Ursula to Christopher Amirant at St Mary in the Marsh in 1729. The Hargrave label may have been printed at any time between 1711 and the death of Benjamin sometime after 1718.

John Robinson of Milden-Hall

Admittedly this is more of a keepsake than a bookplate (F25279), but cannot be, in the year 1732, an ice-printing. The large decorative cartouche or factotum used is similar but not identical to that of a similar production for William Coventry of East Illsley, Berks. The latter, however, commemorated the subject's birth on 28 February 1739 and was printed on the ice at Queenhithe nearly a year later on 29 January 1740 during the great frost fair.

One can assume that Milden Hall near Monks Eleigh is intended, rather than the town of Mildenhall itself. The identification of John Robinson is difficult, unless he is a fairly short-term tenant of John Canham at the Hall and later lived at Denston Hall. The words 'Pray Pay Ye Bearer' below one group of gardening putti implies that the factotum was originally intended to frame bank drafts.

(56%)

The Hare family of Stow Bardolf and Docking

The ever-querulous Norfolk genealogist Walter Rye, enjoyed writing in his *Norfolk Families* (1913): 'Of all the preposterous pedigrees which sprang from the fertile brains of Elizabethan heralds none is so bad as that usually said to belong to this family'. I will not continue the quotation, for Rye's Hare pedigree is hopeless, omitting altogether the owner of the following grand Jacobean armorial (F13751, see cover illustration).

Sir Thomas Hare of Stow Bardolf succeeded his brother Sir Ralph as 4th Bart in 1732 and dated his bookplate two years later when he married Rosamund, daughter of Charles Newby Esqr of Hooton, Yorks, and could impale his arms with hers. He lived until 1760, leaving only two daughters, so was succeeded by his brother George, who died unmarried. The baronetcy passed through the female line, eventually to Thomas Leigh of Iver, Bucks whose grandson Thomas claimed and was given the title in 1818 on changing his surname and arms. His armorial is F13752.

At least one esquire of the Docking branch used a dignified Chippendale armorial with an empty motto scroll (F13742). It would be good to consult Rye, but he is equally unrevealing about the owners of this fine plate. According to him, Hugh Hare, 1st Lord Coleraine, was father of the Hon. Hugh Hare of Docking, who clearly liked to show his 'Esquire' status as well.

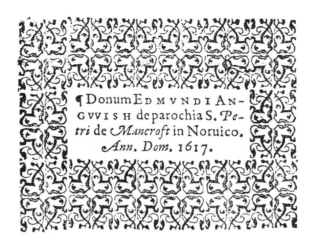

¶ Donum Ed m v n d i An-
g vv i s h de parochia S. Petri de *Mancroft* in Noruico.
Ann. Dom. 1617.

Anguish and Allin

These two names became interlinked in eighteenth century Suffolk, for the usual reason, in order to preserve an inheritance, and the Allins adopted the Anguish arms in the process. Thomas Allin of Blundeston and Somerleyton (1612–85, see *ODNB*) was a successful naval commander in the Dutch Wars, knighted and promoted admiral in 1665. He left only a daughter Alice married to Edmund Anguish of Moulton, Norfolk. Their son Richard, who married Francis Ashurst, changed his name to Allin on being made a baronet in 1699 and died in 1725. Their sons Thomas and Ashurst (the latter in orders) succeeded as second and third baronets. Sir Richard's brother Edmund, who married Mary Betts of Yoxford, remained an Anguish as did their son Thomas (1700–63) who was rector of Halesworth from 1724 (see *The People of a Suffolk Town*, Michael and Sheila Gooch, published by the authors, Halesworth, 1999, page 48). He, like Sir Thomas Allin, 3rd Bart was a subscriber to the apothecary John King's *Essay on Hot and Cold Bathing* in 1737. These two men owned Jacobean armorials: Allin's is T * A (F405) and Anguish a rare Jacobean armorial found in the Viner collection in two states (neither in Franks): V89 with a grotesque below the shield and V90 with a female face. Later the rector moved on to a larger Chippendale armorial (F553).

Long before, Edmund Anguish of Norwich ordered a beautiful typographic label to mark a copy of Whitaker's *Opera Theologica* (Geneva, 1610, 2 vols in one) for presentation to St Peter Mancroft church in 1617 (now City Library Bh.18). Edmund's father Thomas, Mayor of Norwich, died in 1657 aged 84. The Norwich and Suffolk branches of the Anguish family have no obvious connection.

The Earles of Heydon Hall and Fountains of Narford

The Earle family was already established at Salle, the parish with a church like a cathedral, in the fourteenth century. The first Erasmus was born in 1590 and thereafter there was an Erasmus in almost every generation. Augustine Earle was the son of one Erasmus, and father of another, and his Jacobean armorial (F9487) is just like that of Sir Thomas Allin (T * A F405, see above). Augustine married Frances Blaicklock in 1726, succeeded his elder brothers at Heydon Hall in 1728 and died in 1762. Augustine Earle was chief magistrate in Holt Hundred.

His son Erasmus was probably about twelve when he was sent to Gresham's School, Holt

Augustine Earle
of Heydon
in the County of Norfolk Esq

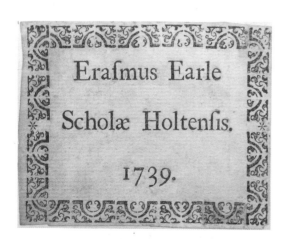

Erasmus Earle
Scholæ Holtensis.
1739.

ADVERSIS · MAJOR · PAR · SECUNDIS

Erasmus Earle
AUL · PEMB · CANTAB.
SOC · COMMENS · 1744

under John Holmes, master there for thirty years from 1730, a polymath who wrote and published the texts he wished his pupils to use in a wide range of subjects (See *ODNB*). Erasmus used printed labels (V1298) to mark his school books, and when he went up to Pembroke Hall in 1744 as a Fellow Commoner, aged 16, he adopted a new armorial, a Jacobean bursting out on the right towards the Chippendale style (V1299). John Holmes' interesting plate made five years before he retired, a tree of Greek verbs, is plate 230 in *British Bookplates*.

Two of Erasmus' male forebears married women of the Fountaine family of Salle. By his time that family had moved to Narford near King's Lynn, where the most celebrated member of the family, Sir Andrew, who took two Grand Tours, furnished his Hall in a manner which attracted many visitors. Born at Salle, and educated at Eton and Christ Church, he graduated in 1697. Chosen by Dean Aldrich to make the Latin oration to William III on his entry to Oxford in 1698, the king knighted him the following year. Sir ANDREW FOUNTAIN's early armorial (V1532), his knighthood denoted by Eq: Aur:, meaning Eques Auratus, has many characteristics of Michael Burghers' work, regarded in his day as the best general engraver in England. The crescent cadency mark is puzzling, since Andrew was certainly his father Andrew's eldest son, but his father had an elder brother and Burghers may have been given the father's arms to copy. From sometime in the 1690s Burghers was appointed *calcographus academicus* to the university. As an arbiter of impeccable taste, none could compete with Fountaine; he became a favourite at the Hanoverian court, and succeeded Sir Isaac Newton as master of the Mint. Sir Andrew died unmarried aged 77 in 1753 and was buried at Narford.

A Jacobean armorial for THOMAS FOUNTAYNE Esq (F1102), on which the neat initials I and F are sometimes written in corrosive black ink, is worth illustrating as a warning that the IGI can seriously mislead. This Thomas (1713–39) and his younger brother John by two years who outlived him, are listed with much accurate information, but they are located at Melton in Suffolk, suggesting that the branch had migrated from Norfolk. In fact they came from Melton-on-the-Hill near Doncaster, and John, who used up his late brother's stock of bookplates, became Dean of York from 1747 to his death in 1802.

Norwich Jacobeans *c.*1730

It is always interesting to stumble on a new East Anglian stock pattern. The style of the name and motto scrolls links the examples so far located and as their owners all lived within easy distance of Norwich, that is where the engraver probably worked. The dates of owners' deaths range from 1732 to 1748, in support of the suggested date above. Taking them in order:

ROBERT CAM'ELL was born in 1693, the eldest son of Robert, attorney of Diss. The family had migrated from Scotland, where their name was probably Campbell, to Gislingham in north Suffolk. Robert took his LL.B at Sidney Sussex College in 1715, LL.D in 1723 (shown on F4931) and held the rectories of Bradwell and Lound for life. In December 1731 he was appointed Lecturer at St Peter Mancroft, an honour he did not long enjoy, for he died the following November. Because Heins made a mezzotint portrait it is likely that he had other claims to fame. Francis Blomefield the historian of Norfolk acknowledged the help he received from Cam'ell. Robert's younger brother William seems not to have gone to Cambridge but had a square fleuron bordered label (F4932). There are two states, differing only in the arrangement of the border ornaments but no examples have been found with other figures added in manuscript than '25' to make the date 1725.

Dr HENRY BRIGGS of Holt was the only son of William, MD and Hannah Hobart his wife of the same place. His armorial (F3717) has the arms of Briggs and Hobart quartered. Hannah's father Edmund's memorial in Holt church (placed by Henry and Hannah) has a memorable inscription 'he had escaped from the malice of the Usurper, who (for his loyalty to the Blessed Martyr, King Charles I) sought after his life and forced him from his paternal

Robert Cam'ell

seat to live in obscurity…'. Briggs and John Holmes, headmaster at Gresham's (see above), collaborated to provide Blomefield with historical materials for his history of Holt Hundred. It was one of Henry's five sons, WILLIAM, who had the plate reworked by changing the first name and removing STP (F3722).

JOHN REDDINGTON, son of another John of Cambridge, was born in 1683. He went up to Trinity in 1698 and took the MA shown on his bookplate (F24704, see overleaf) in 1705. He was a competent High Master of Norwich Grammar School from 1732 to 1737 and spent his last few years at Hethel where he was buried in 1739.

One further example may belong here. It is the armorial without crest of ROBERT MARTIN (1688–1740), attorney of Thetford, elder brother by ten years of 'Honest' Tom Martin of Palgrave. Thomas, employed by Robert as his clerk, disliked the law and neglected it for East Anglian history and topography; he never afforded his own ex-libris, nor has he been detected in using his late brother's armorial by alteration. Two features seem to link this plate (F19868) to that of Joseph Reddington: the open-mouthed grotesque mask above, and the name scroll below.

Beaupré Bell of Outwell

The impressive Jacobean armorial of bold execution for Beaupré Bell (1704–1745) (F2084, see hand-coloured example Plate IV) could tentatively be suggested as another piece of Thomas Hillyard's work (*See SNXL*, 22–32, 38). Bell also used two crest plates (both NIF), one dated 1728, for which no Levi or Hillyard parallels can be suggested. Bell was the last of the line living at Beaupré Hall in Outwell, north-west Norfolk where his father and namesake had kept a herd of at least 500 unbroken horses running wild in the park, some of them over thirty years old. Mother was an Oldfield of Spalding, hence the quarterings. After Westminster and Trinity, Cambridge, the younger Beaupré devoted himself to antiquities, building collections which he bequeathed to his old college. He gave Blomefield considerable help with his great history of the county but although he began many projects he finished few of them.

Beaupré senior allowed a fine library to decay, the books destroyed by damp and mould, but obviously his son cared for their replacements. He was a great one for annotating his books using several elegant hands. In 1737 he presented John Lewis's *Life of Wyllyam Caxton* on publication to the Spalding Gentlemen's Society, and the hand-coloured armorial (see Pl. IV) shown is inscribed to 'Societati Gen: Sti Petri de Burgo In Com: Northampt'. The club, founded in 1710 by the Revd Timothy Neve, was affiliated to the London Society of Antiquaries in 1722, but in the 1740s became the Peterborough Book Society.

VIAM AFFECTAT OLYMPO

Beaupræi Bell
De Beaupré-Hall in
COM: NORFOLC.

Bibliothecae et Societati de
Spalding in Com Lincoln.
D.D.
Beaupré Bell
Ineunte Anno
1740.

Hobart of Blickling

The ex-libris marking some of over 12,000 books in the library at Blickling Hall are the least important reason for visiting it. The ceiling of the Long Gallery (123 feet long) with its display of emblems in plaster made in 1620 alone justifies the journey and the climb to the top of the house.

However, since only the earlier Hobart armorial is in the Franks collection, and together they demonstrate the progress from Baron to Earl, they are worth illustrating. Sir John Hobart 5th Baronet was created 1st Baron Hobart a year after his first wife died in 1727. He remarried in 1728, but the single arms may indicate that the plate (F14891) was commissioned while he was a widower. The motto means 'The giver makes them valuable'.

He was created 1st Earl of Buckinghamshire in 1746 but the second armorial is for his son John who succeeded as 2nd Earl on his father's death in 1756. In 1770, he married as his second wife, Caroline Connolly, and her arms are shown on the sinister shield accollé. The Earl was ambassador to St Petersburg 1762–65, Lord Lieutenant of Ireland 1777–80, and died in 1793.

Wodehouse of Kimberley

Sir Armine Wodehouse succeeded his father John as 5th baronet in 1754. He married Letitia, daughter and coheir of Sir Edmund Bacon of Garboldisham, was MP for Norfolk 1737–68 and died in 1777. His armorial (F32318) may, like the larger F32322, have been engraved by W.H. Toms. Walter Rye in his *Norfolk Families* (1913), pp 1021–23, comprehensively demolishes the Agincourt myth which the family used as motto, since the John Wodehouse who died in 1431, although a courtier, was a man of business and not a fighting man.

Armine's son John was created Baron Wodehouse of Kimberley in 1797, but it was his son and namesake who, before he succeeded in 1834, used the spade shield armorial (F32320) with his wife's Norris arms in pretence. In 1838 he adopted a new plate (F32313) with crest and baron's coronet.

Their son John the third Baron (born 1826) was created Earl of Kimberley in 1866 and F.C. Montagu designed and made the striking crest and earl's coronet plate (F32317). Unsigned, neither Gambier-Howe nor Viner knew the attribution to Montagu.

James of Norfolk

This anonymous Jacobean armorial (F16292, above opposite) so strongly resembles that of James Fysh of King's Lynn; signed by Ben Levi (SNXL, 28), that it is tempting to attribute it to that artist or Thomas Hillyard with whom there were links.

The mother of Sir Henry Tindal Methold, amateur designer and producer of many bookplates (*See SNXL*, 142–43) was Ellen James, eldest daughter of the Revd Edward James, vicar of Hindringham, Norfolk, and that family claimed descent from the James of this bookplate, the vicar using copies by adding his name in manuscript.

Patrick St Clair

R.W. Ketton-Cremer's delightful *Country Neighbourhood*, published in 1951, consists entirely of the letters which the Revd Patrick St Clair wrote to his friend and patron Ashe Windham between 1729 and 1741. St Clair, a Scotsman by birth (in the year before the restoration of the monarchy), spent most his life in the depths of the north Norfolk countryside. Already seventy years of age when the correspondence began, he lived to be 96. The letters were at Felbrigg Hall when Ketton-Cremer's great-grandfather bought it in 1860, and his book richly rewards more than one reading. His Jacobean bookplate arms on F25940, Argent a cross engrailed gules, suggest

The Rev.ᵈ Mᵣ Pat.ˢᵗ Clair

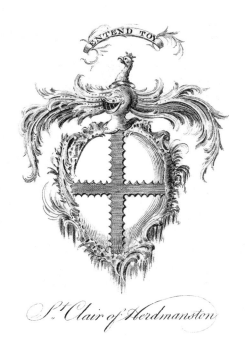

Sᵗ Clair of Herdmanston

that his family claimed descent from the Sinclairs of Herdmanston in Berwickshire (F25937, with the same motto, shown here from a book published in Amsterdam in 1735).

His father John Sinclar was a moderate Presbyterian, a notable figure in the Church of Scotland, whose manse at Ormiston became a school while his sons were growing up. The Marquis of Lothian boarded as a fellow pupil. When Patrick and his brother changed the spelling of their name to St Clair we do not know. Patrick probably finished his education at one of the Dutch universities; he was a good Latinist who took Anglican orders in 1676.

He first began his lifelong connection with the young Norfolk squire Ashe Windham, then aged nineteen, in 1691, proving the greatest assistance two years later, when, coming of age, the full burden of the estates fell on the young man's shoulders. He lived at the Hall, and Ashe presented him to the living of Aylmerton to which the bishop added Thurgarton in 1701.

It was a coincidence that in 1709 both men married, the squire of thirty-seven and the clergyman of fifty. Now the St Clairs settled in the Old Hall in Sustead, midway between Patrick's two parishes, and there their daughter Betty was born in 1711. Elizabeth St Clair succumbed to a terrible fever when Betty was eighteen, so, rather like the bachelor Norfolk parson James Woodforde whose niece Nancy kept house for him, Patrick St Clair spent the rest of his life with the support of his only child.

Mackworth, engraver of King's Lynn

Bookplates by the mid-18th century engraver Mackworth of King's Lynn are surprisingly numerous but uncommon. Fincham lists four signed examples, of which the slender Chippendale armorial for JOHN DINHAM (1725–1782, NIF, V1184) is the first of a stock pattern. The brackets on the delicate rococo frame hold an inkwell with quill and a book and these seem to one of Mackworth's trademarks. The family seems to have originated at Soham, Cambs, in the 16th century, multiplying rapidly in Lincolnshire later. The large engravings

Mackworth made of the architect Henry Bell's buildings in King's Lynn are listed by Samuel Woodward in his *Norfolk Topographer's Manual*. In the search for the engraver's elusive Christian name, Anthony Pincott suggests credibly that he may have been the Henry Mackworth who advertised his own mathematical table for sale in the *Norwich Mercury* for 11 January 1755.

Dinham was the son and younger brother of Spalding physicians; after Eton and Emmanuel (MA 1750), he became perpetual curate of Whaplode Drove and lecturer of Spalding, then from 1759 until his death vicar there and president of the Gentlemen's Society. When Rousseau visited the town, he met and conversed with Dinham at the White Hart Inn. Dinham has a mural monument in the chancel of the church he served for over twenty years.

Two more plates featuring the quill, inkpot and book are probably Mackworth's work. One is for Christ's College, Cambridge (NIF), illustrated in the author's 'William Stephens of Cambridge', *BJ*, March 2005, 4. The other is for THOMAS CASE of Lynn, attorney and common council man who died in 1793, aged 63 (NIF). Thomas, a fourth son according to the martlet on his plate, lived at Testerton House, Great Fransham and married Martha Mallett, accounting for the impalement.

The HARDY Chippendale so strangely bearing Mason arms and crest (F13705) strongly resembles the Dinham plate in several ways. The book and the pen and inkpot are missing, and the brackets are empty. The Masons of Necton and the Hardys of Letheringsett bore quite different arms. No Hardy Mason can be traced, so perhaps a Mason changed surname but not arms. The plate could have been engraved and proofed, then discarded as the arms were wrong. What seems certain is that Mackworth is the artist.

JOSIAH BIRCH, perhaps too grand for inkpots, has urns and garlands instead. This large family migrated from Lincolnshire to Watlington in Norfolk apparently for the shooting. The motto means 'Fair as the flower'.

JOHN TOWERS ALLEN, born about 1744 at Terrington, son of John Allen, gent. After Bury St Edmunds grammar school and St John's, Cambridge (MA 1769), he was rector of Barwick St Mary from 1783 to 1788, the ruins of which church are in the parish of Stanhoe. His plate (F379) is a Jacobean armorial, *c*.1750, with the arms and crest of Towers rather than Allen. The motto means 'Virtue the best defence'.

JENKIN MATHER LEET had a Chippendale trophy armorial (F17955) which Paul Latcham illustrates and describes in his *Bookplates in the Trophy Style*, (2006), plate 051 on page 51. According to Fincham, Barth[olome]w. Middleton had a Chippendale of *c*.1770 signed Mackworth, but it is yet to be located.

One more signed Mackworth plate, for ROBERT HAMILTON of Lynn, is his most remarkable. The only known copy is in the Perez collection. It is very similar to the pictorial Chippendale for John Walford, surgeon of Chelmsford, (NIF), signed Yates and dated 1754, but which plate came first? Hamilton was born in Edinburgh in 1721 and spent the rest of his life in Lynn from 1748 until his death in 1793. A physician, in 1766 he became MD of St Andrews, after which he would surely have used the title. He was also FRS and FRCP. Mackworth's engraving executed between 1748 and 1766 is certainly more delicate than Yates's.

Two more members of the Allen family of Lynn have armorials which are, in different ways, suggestive of Mackworth's work. STEPHEN ALLEN was third of six of the name in succession, and by his wife Elizabeth had Stephen, DD and vicar of Lynn. After her husband died, Elizabeth Allen married Dr Charles Burney the musician in secret in 1767 and became Fanny the diarist's stepmother. Stephen's Jacobean armorial is F387. BAGGE ALLEN's large Chippendale is NIF. He, MD and surgeon of Swaffham, was son of William Allen and his wife Elizabeth, daughter of John Bagge Esq, mayor of Lynn.

ROB.^T HAMILTON

JOHN WALFORD
Surgeon, Chelmsfford, 1754.

Four Jacobean armorials with upward stretching carytids

These plates, three of them for East Anglian clients, are illustrated with the suggestion that they originate from the same workshop, probably in London.

ELISHA BISCOE (1705–76; F2623) is without obvious links to the east, and although he entered Lincoln's Inn, there is no record of him at the Inner Temple. He had estates in Jamaica and in 1754 built Spring Grove, the house in which Sir Joseph Banks later lived.

Closely similar in style, but better engraved, is that of FREDERICK ALPE of Framlingham (NIF, V73) whose father Edward has a mural monument in that church. Frederick died in 1726, aged 56.

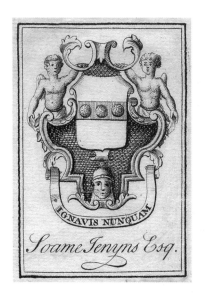

SOAME JENYNS Esq of Bottisham Hall near Cambridge (1704–87; F16421) was of St John's College, Cambridge and a published author. Looking at the three dates of death, Alpe must have had his plate late in life and the others earlier.

WILLIAM BROWNE MD, the eminent and eccentric physician (1692–1774; F4084) was of Durham, but after graduating at Peterhouse he was in 1716 licensed by the University of Cambridge to practise medicine at King's Lynn and stayed there for over thirty years. In 1748 he was knighted through the influence of the duke of Montagu and the following year moved to Queen Square, Bloomsbury. His bookplate is, therefore, pre-1748. An upholder of university-qualified doctors over licentiates, some of the latter embarrassed him by invading a meeting he was chairing while president of the Royal College of Physicians, and he resigned. He was often caricatured with his muff, his spyglass and copy of Horace, to which he was so attached that it was buried with him at Hillington, Norfolk where his own Latin epitaph can be read.

Three more William Stephens ex-libris

Since the article on this Cambridge engraver was published in the *Bookplate Journal* for March 2005, three more interesting examples of his work have been found. Creffield's (NIF) could be for a scholar or fellow of St John's, but its owner was neither, just a playboy. The Scott label (F26332) begins a new group, the engraved festoons resembling those in Colonel Clarke's plate here (F5917) and on Thomas Fauquier's armorial (NIF).

PETER CREFFIELD was born in Colchester in 1719, the son of a wealthy alderman of the town. For eight years he boarded at Ipswich School, going up to St John's College, Cambridge in 1736. Peter was only three when his father Ralph died, and his mother was soon married again to Charles Gray, MP for Colchester in five parliaments and owner of Hollytrees, the splendid house next door to the Castle, which was also his.

Peter was heir to his grandfather, Sir Ralph Creffield from the time his widowed grandmother

died in 1734, and Charles Gray, as his guardian, was steward of the income from several estates in north-east Essex from which Peter's expenses at Ipswich and Cambridge were paid. Accounts and notebooks remain in Essex Record office (ERO D/DRc).

Edward Leeds, Master at Ipswich, had good reason to overlook Peter's lack of promise, for he could charge a boarder what he liked. What Charles Gray paid for Peter each year doubled Leeds' £25 annual stipend, and presumably other boarders were as lucrative. Peter was nine on arrival, thirteen when he succeeded his grandfather Sir Ralph in estates at Mersea and elsewhere and seventeen when he left for Cambridge. He wore a wig from the age of fourteen and was shaving two years later.

Peter was totally unfitted to study at Cambridge to judge from the mispelt notes his tutor James Tunstall forced him to take at one of their interviews:

> That Mr Tunstall wrote to my papar [stepfather] [the letter] that I read November the 5th 1737. He said that I lay a bed all the morning and would not ware a band [bands] but when I did it was so that nobody could see it: & that I never came in to the hall: and that I go out of colledge with out Leave & that I kept the worst company in the colledge; & that Pool[e] was my intamate friend & that I never came to chapel & that I never wore my proper gown & that he would not in the future let me

Alured Clarke D.D.

Colonel Clarke
GODMANCHESTER.

W.ᵐ Scott,
Cambridge.

go out of colledge with out him or some of the fellows at the college and never by my self and he calls Mr Cardale to witness all the forementioned things & he desired my papar that I might not have a servant att coll: without [unless] he was an old one & desired that I might have a [better] self quaintance [knowledge].

It seems astonishing that the dons were prepared to accompany Peter on his excursions, but perhaps they too coveted the bright lights. Peter soon found a usefully rich girlfriend: 'Borrowed of my Dear Creature £18 8 0', hired a violin, engaged a French Horn Tutor and adopted the maxim:

> They may be false who Languish and complain
> But they who part with money never feign

COLONEL CLARKE was the Alured Clarke, gent., (1659–1744) who was prominent in Godmanchester and is commemorated, describing his sons' achievements, on a mural monument in the north aisle of the parish church of St Mary the Virgin there. The crest on the memorial corresponds with that on the armorial, but its shield below is unhelpfully blank. Franks identifies both quarterings as Clarke coats, and the first, according to Burke, has Irish origins. Thus his parents will have belonged to different Clarke families. His second son Alured, DD, Dean of Exeter, used a Jacobean-Chippendale armorial (F5902) with the second Clarke coat only; he died in 1742 (see *ODNB*).

WILLIAM SCOTT is too common a name in mid-18th century Cambridge to make it possible to identify the owner of this label, but it interesting to see that Stephens was prepared to engrave other than armorials (and of course that beautiful Harbord Harbord label (F13654)).

Blackwell of Sprowston, Norwich

The first Sir Lambert Blackwell, MP and diplomat of Surrey, was created a baronet in 1718. His son Sir Charles died in 1741 and the third baronet and the second Sir LAMBERT BLACKWELL, died unmarried in his Sprowston, Norwich, estates in 1801. He had, however,

enjoyed three fine ex-libris: a Chippendale armorial (F2714), a label by George Bickham (F2715) and a spade shield festoon (F2716). No connection has been made with the Ebenezer Blackwell (d.1782, see *ODNB*) whose square Jacobean allegorical appears in *SNXL*, 45.

Putti at work and play

THE FLUDYER BROTHERS, Blackwell Hall Factors. Rarely do putti do anything useful, but one of those on Sir Samuel Fludyer's Chippendale (F10823) has neatly secured a bale of woollen cloth, and marked it with the letters F over ST. Samuel and Thomas Fludyer were sons of another Samuel, a Somerset and London merchant, and his wife Elizabeth de Monsallier.

The elder brother Samuel, was of Lee Place, Kent, alderman and sheriff of London, knighted in 1755 and created a baronet four years later. He was lord mayor of London in 1761–62, at which time the king honoured his brother Thomas with knighthood. He was twice married and had two sons by his second wife Caroline Brudenell who outlived him when he died in 1768, purchasing and improving Langer Lodge for her son and grandson, formerly the Felixstowe home of the querulous Philip Thicknesse when Lt Governor of Landguard Fort, some two miles south.

Sir Samuel's brother Sir Thomas took over his elder brother's copper and had it printed with the name erased, adding his own flourish of a signature instead (F10824). The motto 'L'Industrie recompense' reflects the prosperity of their joint international trade.

Two medical men named MOSES GRIFFITH are conflated in the original *DNB* and a partial attempt at separating them has been made in *ODNB*. The pictorial armorial (F12885) with relaxing putti for Moses Griffith MD is probably for the main subject of that article and not for his namesake of Shrewsbury. The main Moses was baptised in 1699 at Melbourn, Cambridgeshire where his father Edward was incumbent, and apprenticed to a Norwich apothecary, Edward Sayer in 1712. By his wife Elizabeth Guyon whom he married in 1724 he had a son Guyon in 1730 who in 1744 was admitted to study at Leiden, the same year that Moses took his MD there. John Bensusan-Butt believed this, but the *ODNB* has the Salopian Moses taking the Leiden doctorate.

Samuel Fludyer

Thomas Fludyer

M. GRIFFITH. M.D.

The Revᵈ John Eade.

Claiming this plate for the east, our Moses long practised in London before moving to Colchester in 1768 and a comfortable house in Head Street where he lived until his death in 1785. He has a slab in St Peter's church. The arms do not help, since they are given in Burke without any indication of county or region. Of course a third Moses was the artist who helped Thomas Pennant on his Welsh tours.

The Revd JOHN EADE had a pictorial armorial (F9475, see previous page) with a putto who is either concentrating hard on his reading or suffering from an attack of the megrims. He was born about 1734 the son of Thomas, a farmer of Saxmundham. After school at Dedham and Emmanuel College, Cambridge, he was ordained at Norwich in 1762. He was curate of Raydon and then vicar of Tannington from 1772 (also Cotton from 1793) until he died in 1811. For his son John the plate was altered omitting 'The Revd' (F9476).

PHILIP LLOYD (1729–90) was dean of Norwich from 1765 for life, an energetic and practical man who worked with Thomas Ivory on a massive renovation of the cathedral. He improved the deanery and the liturgy did not escape his attention either. His allegorical pictorial (F18495) was probably the design if not the execution of his wife Joyce, for some windows installed in the late 1770s were hers. The motto 'Sfortunato non infidele' means Untoward not unfaithful.

Robert Rogers of Bury St Edmunds

This man's typographic label dated 1760 (F25413) is similar to the Cullum label of the same date (F7538) shown on *SNXL*, 66, and was probably printed by William Green, established in the town since 1758.

The coat of arms in the Chippendale armorial with three roebucks trippant was used by Rogers of Walsham-le-Willows, not far for Bury. Robert, the eldest of three sons of Peter Rogers, silversmith of Bury, entered the Grammar School there in 1745. He died in 1788, aged 51 and was buried, like his father three years later, in the Great Churchyard. It seems probable that he joined his father in the business, and his engraved armorial and small label (both NIF) have all the characteristics of silversmith's work.

Dey Syer of Great Waldingfield

This man's Jacobean armorial (F28702) is engraved in similar style to the last, but could be as many as twenty years earlier and the work of the firm in Peter Rogers' time. There are ample Syer links with Bury St Edmunds. Born second son of Dey Syer of Little Waldingfield in 1721, Dey junior was educated at Lavenham School, then for seven years at Bury Grammar School under Kynnesman before entering Caius College in 1739. The C.C.C. after his name would usually mean Corpus Christi College, but must here be for Caius College, Cambridge.

After graduating and becoming a deacon in 1743, Dey married Elizabeth, daughter of Dr Blomefield of Badingham and held many livings in Norfolk and Suffolk including Kedington, Badingham and Little Waldingfield where he was buried in September 1800.

Great Yarmouth antiquaries

In his very short life, JOHN IVES (1751–76) had time to earn reputations for dalliance, for collecting anything old and for heraldic scholarship for which he was made Suffolk Herald Extraordinary in 1774. The anonymous 'Momus', writing in the *Town and Country Magazine* for September 1771, parodied Ives as 'Curiosus' 'who has spent the last three years in the unvaried pursuit of every appearance of age, and can tell within a month the date of a coin from the weight of its metal, or the age of a manuscript from the dust on its cover.'… 'He ushers you into a room entirely filled with scraps of antiquity and enjoys your admiration with the most heartfelt satisfaction.'…'He is now employed in counting the number of Roman bricks in the wall of Burgh-castle, to add, by way of an appendix, to his elaborate treatise *On the Durable Mortar of the Ancients…*'

He married in 1773, published his account of Burgh Castle, or *Garianonum* the following year, but for his planned *History of Lothingland* only notes and some etched plates (his own) remain.

Ives knew the Yarmouth bookseller and printer SAMUEL KITTRIDGE of Old Broad Row very well and did not admire his productions. When in 1770 Kittridge published *The Theological Quack* or *Falsehood Detected*, Ives wrote to a friend:

> Samuel Kittridge, hatter and hosier, has lately put out a pamphlet entitled *The Theological Quack*, the entire produce of his teeming brain, in which lofty terms, sounding words, ill spelling, and worse grammar fall foul of a fellow that nobody ever heard of till now, one Jonathan Saul, a Methodist preacher of Lastingham. I will shortly contrive a method to send you this curious performance, and then you will be able to judge for yourself of its extraordinary merits.

Samuel died in 1780, his wife Rose before him, aged 49, in 1764. There was a tablet to her and seven of their children in the Baptist chapel. Samuel must not be confused with Samuel of Lowestoft who was roughly contemporary but died in 1766 aged 42 and was married and buried at the parish church there. The bookseller's armorial (F17276, see previous page) has oblique hatchings, wrong for a sable ground, and the motto needs translation: 'Ne pars sincera trahetur:' 'Let naught that is good be lost'.

THOMAS BARBER was for over forty years a clerk in the Customs House at Yarmouth, a job which gave him the leisure and opportunity to form collections of books, coins, antiquities and autographs. Barber was an invaluable assistant to Henry Swinden whose history of the town, published in parts by John Crouse in Norwich, was incomplete when the author died in 1772, leaving John Ives to superintend the completion of the work and write a preface.

Barber, reserved and eccentric, died intestate, leaving £2,000 in a box in his bedroom and such curios as 'a piece of Queen Elizabeth's coronation robe, of flower-crimson satin, wrought with silver and gold'. His Chippendale armorial bookplate (F1406) has one Greek and one Latin

T. BARBER

Φιλαϱχαι℗

NORFOLCIENSIS

word; *Philarchios Norfolciensis* means just 'antiquary of Norfolk'. If he was entitled to the coat of arms he sprang from north Suffolk, perhaps from Fressingfield, where the Whittingham Hall family preferred the spelling BARBAR and used the same coat with crest of a bull's head out of ducal coronet.

JAMES BARBAR marked his father Robert's subscription copy of John Kirby's *Suffolk Traveller* (second edition, 1764) with his neat Chippendale armorial (NIF). He spelt the family surname Barber in the will he made in 1808, dying the following year.

Griffith Davies of Harwich

GRIFFITH DAVIES senior was, between 1743 and 1776, fifteen times mayor of Harwich. Obviously of Welsh stock, his parents Thomas and Mary had him baptised at Epping on 25 August 1722, and he married Elizabeth Goodacre on 24 April 1747 at Theydon Garnon. They had come to East Anglia to stay. Their family was well spread out, two boys christened at Theydon Garnon and a girl and a boy at North Weald, all between 1749 and 1766, the last Griffith junior on 10 November that year. The Jacobean armorial for Griffith senior (F8104) has impaled arms. Griffin junior, also of Harwich, quartered his parents' arms in his Chippendale (NIF), but quartered his father's coat with another second and fourth. The crest is a wolf passant and the Welsh motto 'Gwell pwill nag aur' means 'Better discretion than gold'. Griffith Davies was a subscriber to the second edition of Kirby's *Suffolk Traveller* in 1764.

The Baileys of Harwich and Ipswich

Two rare plates for this father (NIF) and daughter (F1152) are credibly dated almost thirty years apart. They have on the shields what passes at first glance for heraldry but it is invaded by names and initials; the symmetry is strict. Yet the charges, even the hatching, are consistent, except that Sarah adopts a chevron, but both state Ipswich as their place of abode. The oddest thing is that Bailey or Baillie coats in Burke's *Armory* include stars (usually nine) and a sun.

One John Bailey of Harwich was a member of the Ipswich British Union Lodge during its founding year, 1762. Two other Harwich men gained brief experience of masonic matters in the same way, returning to use their knowledge in founding the first lodge in Harwich. If the mock heraldry were masonic, the significance of the initials MO on John's plate cannot be elucidated, and surely Sarah should have devised something quite different.

Nathaniel Turner Esq of Stoke Hall, Ipswich

The strange thing about this Chippendale pictorial is that it is known only from a modern (*c.*1900) reprint preserved in the W.H. Booth collection in the Suffolk Record Office at Ipswich. Booth was in his day renowned for his collection of Chippendale armorials, and if he couldn't find an original print presumably no one could. Booth notes that the print came to him in March 1920 from a Mrs Holt-Wilson, then in Canada, whose father, a Turner of Tuddenham Hall, had the original copper. It goes without saying that it is not in Franks. The heraldry also presents a difficulty, since the coat quartered with Turner is not listed in Papworth or Corder. Without the chaplet in chief it could be for Worthington of Suffolk. Turner married Elizabeth Tylden of Wye in Kent, explaining the impaled arms. D.E. Davy gives the crest for Turner of Stonham Aspal. The pictorial part of the design makes the plate into an agricultural trophy.

Benjamin Page Grimsey's *Monograph on the Parish of St Mary Stoke, Ipswich*, 1885–87, provides a little more about the family at Stoke Hall from about 1764. The Revd Cuthbert Douthwaite came as rector in 1751 and had to answer diocesan queries in the mid-1760s. 'The parish... consists chiefly of farmhouses and is one of the suburbs of Ipswich, containing sixty families. There is one family of note: *viz*: Nathaniel Turner Esq. Advertised to let in the *Ipswich Journal* on 6 November 1753, the Hall was described as a commodious, handsome brick house, a large hall, three parlours, a good kitchen and servants' hall. Turner did his duty as one of the overseers of the parish five times between 1766 and 1788, but was never churchwarden, and sons were baptised in 1769 and 1795. The family spent most of the rest of the century there.

Custance, Beauchamp Proctor and Collinson

The diarist parson James Woodforde, who arrived as rector of Weston Longville in 1776, enjoyed entirely cordial relations with his Squire, John Custance of Weston House, and his wife Frances, daughter of Sir WILLIAM BEAUCHAMP-PROCTOR, 1st Baronet of Langley Park, near Norwich (1722–73; F24233). He publicly or privately named (christened) their many offspring and was handsomely rewarded for his pains with guineas and hospitality. John's brother Press Custance gets a mixed character in the diaries. John's grandfather and namesake was a linendraper of St Andrew's, Norwich, who, after being twice mayor of the city, bought the Weston estate in 1726. His wife Sarah was a Hambleton, the name they gave their eldest son who, as Hamble, entered Corpus Christi, Cambridge in 1733. He took no degree, studying for the law instead at Lincoln's Inn and marrying Susanna, daughter of John Press, another Norwich alderman. Hamble may have had a Jacobean armorial bookplate with just HC before

Moyles Henry Custance.

Lith. Daveluy. Bruges

he went up to Cambridge (F7737), for it occurs with and without the manuscript addition of the rest of his surname and the college initials CCCC; it is a very early ribbon festoon.

Squire John, who succeeded to the estate on his father's death in 1757, used a fine but anonymous Chippendale (F7738). The engraved copper for this plate is in the Pincott collection. What is hardly mentioned in the diaries is that, far from living exclusively on his country estates, John Custance held office as one of the Gentlemen of the Privy Chamber.

There are two more Custance armorials of interest. One for Frances (F7736) has Custance quartered with Custace (a long-standing heraldic mistake for Hambleton in the family's use of arms) impaling Bacon quarterly. Frances was the wife of Sir Hambleton Francis Custance, the squire's grandson, and daughter of Sir Edmund Bacon of Garboldisham. (Bacon quartering Quaplode was used by Sir Nicholas Bacon, Lord Keeper of the Great Seal, on the earliest known gift plate in books he presented to Cambridge University in 1574.) A granddaughter Olive, briefly married to Lord Alfred Douglas (Wilde's Bosie), has one of the two most beautiful bookplates ever made, in the view of the artist Aubrey Beardsley (see *BJ*, NS, 4, p.10 and back cover).

Myles Henry Custance was Sir Hambleton's brother and his armorial was lithographed in Bruges about 1840 by Daveluy. In about 1842 he married Georgiana Collinson, fifth daughter of Charles Streynsham Collinson of the Chantry, Sproughton, near Ipswich and their arms are impaled. Georgiana's father (F6472) and grandfather Michael (F6469) had stylistically similar festooned spade shield armorials, the shields suspended from bows through rings. The latter died in 1795 aged 67 and the former in 1831 aged 78. Michael's father Peter was a noted antiquary and naturalist (see *ODNB*) whose library was sold at auction in 1834.

AT THE
CHANTRY, NEAR IPSWICH.

A CATALOGUE

OF THE

VALUABLE LIBRARY,

ENGRAVINGS,

Books of Prints, Drawings, and Paintings.

OF THE LATE

CHARLES S. COLLINSON, ESQ.

CONSISTING OF

THE WORKS OF THE BEST AUTHORS,

IN GENERAL LITERATURE,

And including the Rare Books in Natural History, collected by the late

PETER COLLINSON, ESQ. F. R. S.

Many of which were Presentation Copies from the Authors,
And Enriched by him, with Marginal Notes, and Illustrated with

ORIGINAL DRAWINGS,

BY EDWARDS, EHRET, BARTRAM, ETC.

A COLLECTION OF PORTRAITS,

AND MISCELLANEOUS PRINTS AND ETCHINGS, BY THE
EARLY ENGRAVERS,

AS ALSO BY

Woollett, Strange, Mason, **Boydell, Hogarth,** *Bromley, &c.*
AND MANY BY THE BEST FRENCH ENGRAVERS.

Boydell's Collection of Prints, the Roman Galleries, &c.
MANY VALUABLE DRAWINGS, BY THE OLD MASTERS,

PENCIL SKETCHES BY RICHARDSON.

And Beautiful Coloured Drawings of Subjects of Natural History.

A VALUABLE

COLLECTION OF PAINTINGS,

INCLUDING SPECIMENS BY

CANALETTI, BERGHEM, POUSSIN, FRANCK, TENIERS, VAN-
GOYEN, W. MARLOW, MONAMI, POWELL, &c.

WHICH WILL BE

SOLD BY AUCTION,

BY

ROBERT GARROD,

AT THE

CHANTRY, NEAR IPSWICH,

On Monday, the 21st day of July, and Six following
days, (Sunday excepted.)

Sale to Commence each Day at Eleven o'clock.

To be Viewed on the Wednesday and Thursday previous to the Sale, by
Catalogues, One Shilling each.

E. SHALDERS, PRINTER, IPSWICH.

1834.

Wymondham ex-libris

BARTHOLOMEW DEY was born in 1702, the son of John Dey, a Norwich weaver, and after school at Wymondham entered Caius in 1720 and graduated MB five years later. Although he was a fellow of Caius for the rest of his life, in 1728 he returned to the market town where he was at school to practise until he died in 1780. The date he became MD is not known but the Chippendale armorial (F8584) was engraved about 1760. The arms are those of the D'Eye family (of Eye, Suffolk); it is doubtful whether he was entitled to them.

JOHN STEPHENSON CANN appears in White's *Directory* of 1845 as solicitor, clerk to the justices and commissioner of taxes. He married Sarah, daughter of William Bircham of Hackford Hall and The Ollands. When Sarah's sister Martha married Guy Lloyd of Bawdeswell Hall in 1807 the Canns lived at Cavick House, described by Pevsner as 'the best house outside Wymondham'. (F5066) Many families used the motto 'live that you may live'. The printed label with just 'ANNE BIRCHAM / Hackford / 1807' is for another of Sarah's sisters who died unmarried.

JOHN CLARKE STOUGHTON was born at East Dereham in 1765, son of Peter Stoughton, solicitor of Wymondham and Elizabeth Clarke his wife. His 'garter' armorial (F28305) is contemporary with the last even if not by the same engraver. He followed his father's profession, but his elder brother James was rector of Foxley and Sparham from 1792 and used a similar armorial with a different motto (NIF). There were no children of John's marriage in 1799 to Hester Payne at Hardingham; after his death in 1806 she married William Mitchell, yet another Wymondham solicitor.

TALBOT of Gonvile's Hall. This armorial (F28855) shows the arms of Talbot, quarterly of 12, as granted in 1584. The bookplate was for the antiquary the Revd THOMAS SUGDEN TALBOT MD, DL (1778–1832), son of Thomas and Frances Ransome Talbot and rector of the Tivetshalls. When in 1803 he married Anne, only daughter of John Hill Esq., of Gressenhall (see *SNXL*, 84), he was also rector of Hempstead with Lessingham. These Talbots were descended from Sir John Talbot of Salesbury, a junior branch of the Talbots of Bushall, Yorkshire. The Revd Talbot is chiefly remembered as friend and collaborator of Dawson Turner (see *ODNB*) to whom he was related, and for his graphite rubbings of brasses in Norfolk churches made when he was still a schoolboy in 1793 and 1794. At Ingham he rubbed brasses sold for their metal in 1799, thus preserving their record. Cotman used Talbot's rubbings when etching plates for *Norfolk Brasses* in 1819, and they include some of the earliest examples in the collection of the Society of Antiquaries of London.

Bartholomew Dey. M:D.
17

John Stephenson Cann.
Wymondham.
NORFOLK.

ANNE BIRCHAM,
HACKFORD.
1807.

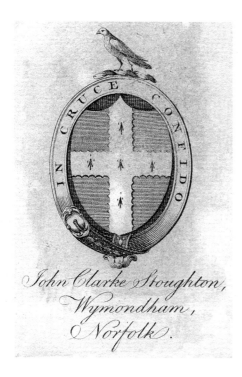

John Clarke Stoughton,
Wymondham,
Norfolk.

Revᵈ James Stoughton,
Sparham,
Norfolk.

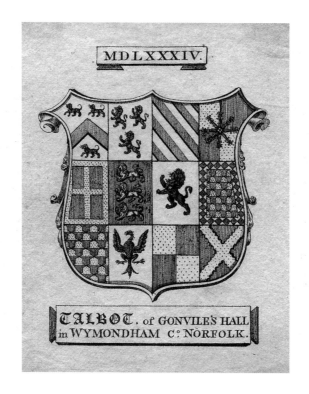

MDLXXXIV.

TALBOT. of GONVILE'S HALL
in WYMONDHAM Cᵒ NORFOLK.

Tyrell Carter of Beccles

This surgeon first made his mark at Beccles when in May 1748 he certified that there were only three houses with smallpox in the town. In 1754 he took on 'a youth well educated and intended for a surgeon and apothecary. He shall if desired be instructed in midwifery in his last year', but needed a new assistant one, two and four years later. He last looked for an apprentice in 1782, and must eventually have sold up and gone to sea, where he died on 26 April 1799 on board 'The Glory' in Lord Bridport's fleet. His Jacobean/Chippendale armorial is NIF.

Nathaniel Carter of London

This Jacobean armorial (NIF, V744), with the same bearings for Carter, may be a little earlier than the last plate. It adds a ninth example of the stock pattern illustrated and discussed in *SNXL*, 28–30. East Anglian links were provided for the first eight, and these Carter arms were also shown for the Norfolk parson Samuel at *SNXL*, 48. The name is far too common to aid firm identification, but two of the name were christened in Wattisfield and Badwell Ash, both Suffolk, in the first decade of the 18th century, and Nathaniel and Francis Carter were wine merchants in Crutched Friars in Kent's 1740 London Directory.

Dickins of Cowlinge

The first Ambrose Dickins Esq, attorney of Covent Garden had sons Ambrose, Francis and George who all came to Suffolk, George to be rector of Little Bradley next door to Cowlinge where Francis was the first to own Branches Park. GEORGE's early and unusual Chippendale armorial (F8626) as a member of Trinity Hall and dated 1739 has some of the characteristics of William Stephens' work. Francis and his wife are shown almost life size seated on their Peter Scheemakers monument in Cowlinge church.

Francis's elder brother AMBROSE junior succeeded him in the property in 1747 and has the Jacobean armorial (F8622) with 1740 and the label for an eldest son. If it were not for the untidy envelope of the shaded area one would suggest John Clark as the engraver. His son FRANCES

(1750–1833) copied his father's plate in 1795, wisely omitting the ragged shading (F8625).

To show and attempt to explain all the Dickins' armorials, the very eccentric F. Dickins plate (F8624) must be included. To judge from the impalement, this Francis married not a wife, but the Regius Professorship of Civil Law at Cambridge. A fellow of Trinity Hall, and LL. D, he held the prestigious chair from 1714 to 1755 when he died. It seems likely that he was a brother of the first Ambrose above.

Samuel Lowell, engraver and minister of the gospel

We can be fairly certain that Samuel designed and engraved his own allegorical pictorial (F18799) for its style follows that of the plates he engraved after Isaac Johnson in Robert Loder's *Account of the Woodbridge Charities*, 1792. It looks rather more a tradecard and may have been used as such.

A Yorkshireman by birth, Samuel came to Woodbridge in 1789 as congregational minister at the Quay Meeting House where he will have been Johnson's pastor, hence the link. He moved to the Independent Chapel in Bridge Street, Bristol in 1799 was there for the rest of his life, dying in 1823. Between 1794 and 1824 eleven of his works were published, the last posthumous statement giving reasons for his dissent from the Church of England. Two stipple engraved portraits of Lowell were published, the earliest in the *Evangelical Magazine* for 1795, the other of 1802 in the *Theological Magazine*. They are correctly titled 'of Woodbridge' and 'of Bristol' respectively.

Johnson Gedge of Bury St Edmunds

JOHNSON GEDGE (1800–1863) had only just left the Grammar School when in 1818 his father Peter died leaving him to edit and publish the *Bury and Norwich Post* at 2 Hatter Street to support his mother Ann (née Johnson) and the family. His father's partner William Barker was still head of the printing business, but Johnson was taken into partnership in 1828, and became sole proprietor in 1834. His three-part book label (F.11769) uses older blocks, a trophy device, his name in open type in a floral frame and a Bewick-style wood engraved tailpiece incorporating the name of the town which strongly resembles one with 'Ipswich' used by George Jermyn on

the title-page of Coyte's *Hortus Botanicus Gippovicensis*. There were many links between printers in the two towns, and the production of a matching pair of tailpieces could have been the idea of the Decks or John Rackham. The central device was also used by WILLIAM FREEMAN of Norwich in 1804 (NIF).

Capel Lofft of Troston and Robert Bloomfield
A Fig for the Heralds

From about 1780 there lived at Troston Hall near Bury St Edmunds the remarkably eccentric leading radical CAPEL LOFFT (1751–1824). His father Christopher Lofft had been private secretary to Sarah, the formidable Duchess of Marlborough, and his mother Anne was the sister of Edward Capell the Shakespearian scholar. After Eton he went up to Peterhouse at Cambridge, where he was influenced by radical theology and politics. Taking no degree, he read for the bar at Lincoln's Inn instead, although he rarely practised as a barrister. There, one of his most important legal achievements was to report a test case which exposed the fact that slavery was not recognised in English law and therefore impossible to legislate against. He was also a strong critic of the government's attempts to re-assert control over the North American colonies by force.

When he inherited Troston Hall from his uncle (according to one commentator it offered him 'comfort and hospitality rather than cold magnificence'), he set about naming almost every tree in the park after his heroes: John Evelyn had a large elm, Homer, Cicero and Milton all had fine specimens, but only a laurel, specially planted, was good enough to honour John Howard the prison reformer who visited him in 1781. By now Lofft had left the Church of England and joined the Unitarians.

Lofft was a natural choice to serve as a county magistrate, but after he failed through official channels to save a poor Hadleigh girl from hanging for a petty theft in 1800, he protested at length on the scaffold. His name was silently removed from the next year's list of justices. His Whiggish ideas and implacable opposition to the younger Pitt had made him the leading reformer in Suffolk and put him beyond the establishment pale. A man before his time, he wanted equality for dissenters, universal male suffrage and the abolition of capital punishment.

It was his opinion of Napoleon Buonaparte whom he idolised which earned him the greatest opprobrium. He always showed his visitors a lock of the emperor's hair kept in a silver casket.

A VIEW NEAR BURY—SUFFOLK.

When the allies arrested Buonaparte in 1815, Lofft took out a writ of Habeus Corpus. The next year at Troston he entertained the Polish officer who had been Napoleon's favourite *aide-de-camp*. The Tory papers were quick to publish such squibs as:

To Capel Lofft
A lock of great Napoleon's hair
With transport filled thy soul;
Oh! what must then thy raptures be
To have his very Pole?

The mezzotint 'View Near Bury – Suffolk' lends support to the writer of his obituary in 1824: 'His figure was small, upright, and boyish; his dress – without fit, fashion or neatness; his speaking – small voiced, long sentenced, and involved; his manner – persevering, but without command.' His detractors accused him of neglecting soap and water. He went abroad with his second wife in 1818 and died near Turin in Italy, but is buried at Troston where there is a dignified mural memorial. On his modest armorial bookplate (F18606) the single arms are those

78

of Capel, although the arms of Lofft of Troston had already been granted in his father's time. He was therefore not to be bound by the rules of heraldry.

ROBERT BLOOMFIELD, the rural poet of *The Farmer's Boy*, was born at Honington in 1766 and his tailor father died before he was one. His mother, the village schoolmistress, now had to spin wool as well to feed her six children. At least she could teach her brood and Robert was soon reading Gray's *Elegy* and the works of Oliver Goldsmith. When he was seven his mother remarried and more children arrived, so Robert was sent to live with a relation at nearby Sapiston. His elder brothers took him to London where he learnt the cobbler's art, but without a proper apprenticeship he risked prosecution. There he 'sold his fiddle and got a wife', Mary-Anne Church, daughter of a Woolwich shipbuilder.

Back in Suffolk he worked on the rural epic which brought him fame. It has four seasonal sections (Autumn contains the line 'The rude inelegance of poverty', to which he was never a stranger). His first patron, Capel Lofft of Troston Hall, found him a publisher for it. By writing a preface for the *Farmer's Boy* Lofft greatly assisted the poet, but it exposed himself to press

ridicule for his efforts. Impressed by the book, Augustus Henry, 3rd Duke of Grafton, awarded Bloomfield a generous pension of £15 a year, which the next Duke, less admiring of cobbler-poets, paid only irregularly.

More collections of poems followed, *Rural Tales* and *Wild Flowers*, and the first contained one of his most popular: 'The Fakenham Ghost'. This is Fakenham Magna nearby, not the Norfolk market town. The first two lines help to explain why Bloomfield is not much read today: 'The lawns were dry in Euston Park; (Here truth inspires my tale)', but we are soon told that 'an ancient dame' was hurrying 'to gain the vale of Fakenham and hail its willow shade'. As it grew dark, 'a short quick step she hears come patting close behind'. 'Now terror seized her quaking frame' and 'she muttered many a prayer'. Yes, you have guessed aright. 'An Ass's Foal had lost its dam within the spacious park; and, simple as the playful lamb, had followed in the dark.' He became, of all things, a household pet and 'his little hoofs would rattle round upon the cottage floor; the matron learned to love the sound that frightened her before'.

Bloomfield never built on the fame *The Farmer's Boy* gave him, and the rest of his life was spent in pursuit of publishers who pocketed his rightful dues and defending himself against accusations of radical tendencies in religion and politics. It has always seemed strange that in 1813 he could apparently afford more than one personal bookplate (F2867) caricaturing many facets of his life. The motto 'A Fig for the Heralds' seems to show what he thought or its designer thought of correct heraldry. When a second device in the same style turned up in the *Journal of the Ex Libris Society* (ix, 1899, 59), it becomes necessary to look for a patron wealthy enough so to indulge the penniless poet, and surely Capel Lofft is our man.

The third 'armorial' here illustrated has never before been connected with Bloomfield, possibly because it is so rare. It is the actual plate used for the illustration in a later volume of the same *Journal* (xvvii, 1907, 165) where it appears as a Bookplate for Identification, No. 619. S.A. Grundy-Newman, the Society's Secretary and Treasurer, pencilled notes on the reverse of the plate used for this illustration, and no one responded with any suggestions. J.P. Rylands

listed it as unidentified, and Viner added with some justice 'not a bookplate'. The 'quarterings' on the three bogus armorials are very similar in content and arrangement, and the mottoes are entirely consistent with the views of Lofft. Only the largest plate is signed, but there are strong grounds for believing that all three are by William Jackson of Gutter Lane, Cheapside.

Late in life, Bloomfield ended a sad letter to his family from London 'Your cheated and bamboozled Father'. Poor health impeded his work in their support and caused his death in 1823 in Bedfordshire. His headstone in Campton churchyard has the epitaph: 'Let his wild native wood notes tell the rest', but his strictures on Suffolk cheese are more memorable: he wrote that even hogs found it 'too big to swallow, and too hard to bite'.

John 'The Scoundrel' Benjafield

As if this man's life were not sufficiently complicated, the ex-libris which he used have many varieties and it is best to begin this account with them.

The Blandford label for John Benjafield of about 1780 is V316. He replaced it with a crest plate first in Dorset, then without location stated and finally Bury St Edmunds. The Franks collection has one without location printed in red and blue (F2189) and one with 'Dorset' printed simply in black (F2190). In the author's collection there are several others: the Dorset crest printed in red blue and yellow (see Plate IV), one with just Benjafield printed in black, and another with the addition of Bury St Edmunds on the next line. The motto 'Despicio terrena' means 'I despise earthly things' and belonged to the Bedingfields of Ditchingham.

The Benjafield eared shield armorial with Argent three cannon balls Sable (NIF) is probably his also. John Benjafield claimed descent from the Bonvilles in the reign of King John and certainly appropriated the crest of Benevile, whose arms are Argent on three pellets as many chevrons of the field, and the armorial is quite close to that.

Edith Anne Greene's pictorial bookplate for herself is shown on page 83 because it depicts the house, built into the ruins of the west front of great abbey of Bury St Edmunds, which became Benjafield's property in 1796.

John Benjafield was christened somewhat tardily on 19 May 1758, the son of William Benjafield at Blandford Forum in Dorset. John died a widower in Bury St Edmunds in 1832, aged 75, his wife Mary Anne Symonds, whom he married in St Mary's church, Bury in 1796 having died in Bath in 1815 aged 46.

In his youth, John was ambitious to be at the centre of affairs. At various times he was one of the king's Yeoman of the Guard, a King's Messenger and Captain in the West Kent Militia. Much later he commanded the Bury Volunteer Infantry. Probably mainly for political reasons (he was a Tory follower of Pitt, and an opponent of the Whigs led by Fox, and the circle of the Prince of Wales) he bought his way into the editorship of the *Morning Post* in 1784 jointly with a colleague who managed the business side.

He claimed that he was pressed to sell his interest in the *Morning Post*, and the business agreement he accepted in 1789 gave him a sizeable annuity. His detractors, however, argued that he had agreed not to publish scandalous information he possessed concerning the Prince

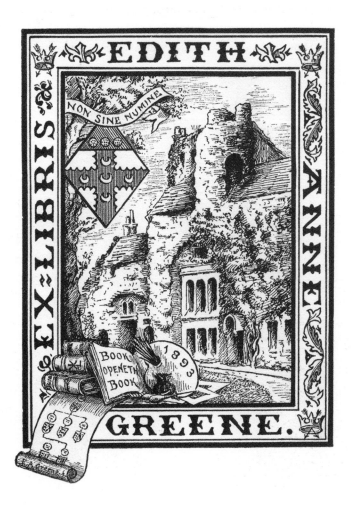

Regent's marriage with Mrs Fitzherbert, and received the annuity by blackmailing these exalted personages through their agents.

All might have been well, had he not tried to oust the Whigs from the corporation and charities of Bury St Edmunds, making many enemies. He became a real thorn in the flesh of James Oakes, the banker and diarist. Some of his enemies wrote letters to the Bury *County Chronicle* which Benjafield considered libellous, and he sued the printer and proprietor in a celebrated case heard at the Guildhall in London before Lord Ellenborough and a Special Jury in December 1812. Benjafield lost and immediately published a statement challenging the verdict and giving a full account of the trial. On balance, since the annuity certainly came from the Duchy of Cornwall, the jury was right.

The scandal of this and another lost libel case did little to lessen Benjafield's ambitions in the town and he remained a Capital Burgess, a county JP unpopular with his colleagues, a governor of the grammar school, the workhouse, and a Guildhall Feoffee.

The involved story of Benjafield's time in Bury, entirely fascinating, is best told by Jane Fiske in the first volume of her *The Oakes Diaries*, pp 136–50 (Suffolk Records Society vol. 32, 1990).

Robert Roe of Cambridge

Amongst makers of die-sinker bookplates, some stand out for the crispness of their productions. Miss Banks' collection (59.148) has Roe's delightful tradecard as engraver and printseller, the view of King's College, Cambridge probably taken from his shop, No. 10, King's Parade. William Wilkins' additions of 1824–28 to the east range seem complete, which gives the card an earliest date. Bookplates are not mentioned, but 'Arms, Crests, Designs &c' are.

Fincham lists seven bookplates by Roe, only two for college libraries, a fine general one for Peterhouse and a bequest plate to Trinity dated 1826. His other recorded plates are all for college men. Josiah Buckland was a fellow of Sidney Sussex and later headmaster of Uppingham, and Edward Richards Adams went up to Caius in 1828. John Hindes Groome, son of Robinson Groome, merchant and mariner of Aldeburgh and his wife Anne, daughter of Robert Hindes, was born there in 1776. After an MA (1801) and a fellowship at Pembroke he held various curacies in Suffolk, but was rector of Earl Soham from 1818 to his death in 1845.

Roe must have been in business well before 1820 as he is featured in a treble acrostic (the author's favourite way of featuring local people and events) in *The Poetical Works of James Chambers, Itinerant Poet*, first published that year. James Chambers, born at Soham in

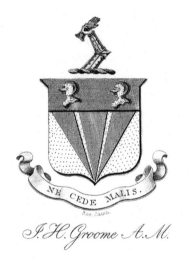

I.H. Groome A.M.

E. Richards Adams, Junr.

Jos. Rowles Buckland, S.T.P.
Sid. Suss. Coll. Cant. Soc.

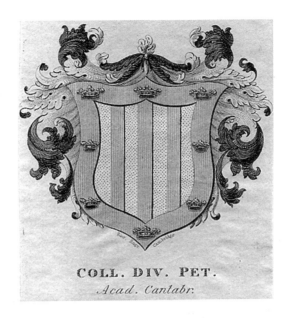

COLL. DIV. PET.

Acad. Cantabr.

ROE,
Engraver, Printseller,
AND FRAME MANUFACTURER.
Opposite King's College.

A SELECT COLLECTION OF PROOFS, AND THE FINEST IMPRESSIONS OF PRINTS BY THE BEST MODERN & ANCIENT MASTERS.

Gentlemen's *Fashionable* Boots & Shoes.
ROE,
Boot & Shoe Maker,
St Clements Fore-street
Ipswich.
Ladies shoes of various colors and the present taste.

TREBLE ACROSTIC.

*(Acrostic for Robert Roe, Printer in Copperplate,
and Engraver, Cambridge).*

A dorn'd superb,	P ellucid rays	A ppear,
C reation shines	R efulgent, far and	N ear,
R esplendent scenes	I n Autumn yield	D elight,
O mnifick power may	N ew applause	E xcite ;
S pring will revive,	T he grand parterre look	N eat,
T hose florid scenes will	E ntertain the	G reat ;
I n Spring the blushing	R ose sheds beauties	R are,
C arnations breathe perfume	I n vernal	A ir ;
F rail man must sure, when	N ature's works he's	V iew'd,
O bey celestial	C alls, each vice	E lude,
R esent all thoughts	O bscene, and converse	R ude ;
R ich gentry, void of	P ride, dear babes	Caress,'
O bedient children	P rize, of meek	A ddress,
B lessings attend, no	E nemies	M olest ;
E namell'd scenes	R evive the languid	B reast :
R ich neat engravings	P olish'd, and	R efin'd,
T o please true friends to	L ove who are	I nclin'd,
R elations at his	A bsence seem	Distrest,
O ld Ipswich friends will	T reat a welcome	G uest,
E ach hour on Christmas	E ve much joy will be	E xprest.

Cambridgeshire in 1748, was the son of an industrious leather-seller, but when he was sixteen he left home, and for over sixty years led a nomadic life, mostly in Suffolk.

Jemmy was happiest sleeping under hedges and in barns, barely supporting himself and his dogs. It may have been when he settled for a time at Earl Soham that he got to know Roe through rector Groome. He died in 1827.

Owen Roe, from at least 1811 until his death in 1825 a boot and shoe maker of St Clement's, Ipswich was perhaps a brother or cousin of Robert, who may have made his tradecard. The acrostic mentions 'old Ipswich friends' and another Owen Roe, perhaps Owen's son, was a copperplate engraver in 1839 and a carver and gilder at 2 Upper Brook Street, Ipswich until his death in 1850.

Samuel Wegg of Colchester

John Bagnall began printing in Ipswich as early as 1720, and the booklabels he made for Deborah Notcutt (a child's keepsake) and for Samuel Pickering, Notary Publick, are dated 1726 and 1731 respectively (see *SNXL*, 108) but it was not until 1734 that John Pilborough, draper and bookseller of Colchester, printed a dated item, a keepsake recording the birth of the eleven year-old Samuel Wegg, already studying at the Royal Grammar School. He was christened at St Nicholas, Colchester on 4 December 1723. The label may at first have read Master Samuel Wegg, for there is an odd space left for a missing word. Two different fleurons are used, one for the top and bottom and the other at the sides, and the only known specimen (at Yale) was badly trimmed and later torn.

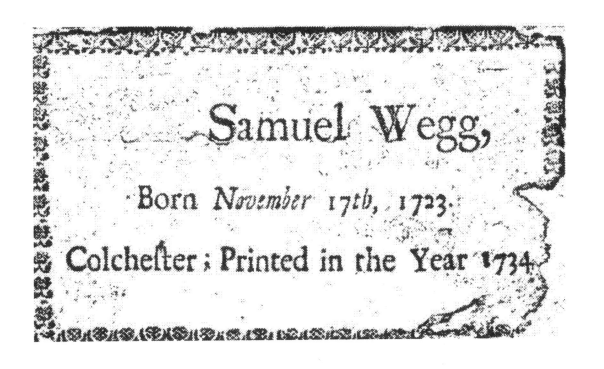

Samuel Wegg,

Born *November* 17th, 1723.

Colchester; Printed in the Year 1734

SAM^L WEGG ESQ^R

Saml Wegg. Esqr

We learn more about Samuel when he was a wealthy barrister, fellow, treasurer and vice-president of the Royal Society, from his later bookplates, an etched Chippendale and a spade shield bookpile (Plate IV shows it printed in colour from Miss Banks' 'Book Tickets', D3.15 in BM Prints and Drawings). The crescent on the Chippendale armorial indicates that he had an elder brother (George, for whom see below) and the arms of Le Hook, Hoop or Heup in pretence record his marriage at Lambeth in 1745 to Elizabeth, elder daughter and co-heir of Benjamin Lehook. The bookpile can hardly be earlier, but its quartered arms show his parents, George Wegg, Freeman of Colchester and Anna Maria Cowper. The motto means 'to have a conscience free from guilt'. Samuel died in 1802 in Acton.

Colchester Libraries

There are no contemporary distinguishing marks in the library which Samuel Harsnett, archbishop of York, bequeathed to the town in his will of 1631 and which is now part of the library at the University of Essex at Wivenhoe.

Charles Gray, five times MP for the town and owner of the castle and Hollytrees, the fine house in the grounds, set up a mainly antiquarian library in the castle in 1749. The next year he formed a book club based on the collection, gentlemen being invited to subscribe and gain the right to borrow. Gifts of books flooded in. After Gray's death in 1782 new members names were put to a ballot, the numbers limited to thirty.

The first bookplate, based on the borough arms, was designed and presented by Gray's fellow antiquary and friend George Wegg (elder brother of Samuel, mentioned above) who initialled and dated it GW ded[it] 1750. He and Gray were both married to daughters of Ralph Creffield. The scroll reads THE GIFT OF [leaving space for the donor's name]

TO THE COLCHESTER LIBRARY, and in the example illustrated the book came from the Revd John, son of William Milton of Dedham, who was vicar of St James's, Colchester from 1743–67.

At the anniversary meeting in 1793 it was ordered: 'that for the more effectual security of the Library Books a Stamp of some device be impressed on the outside of every book… to be a representation of Colchester Castle cut in brass with these words inscribed in the compartment, viz. Colchester Castle Society'. The treasurer that year paid one guinea to 'Mr Dunthorne for a drawing of the castle – a device for a brass tool for stamping the Library Books' and twice as much to Mr Timbury who made the brass tool. James Dunthorne senior (1730–1815) was the artist concerned as at that time his son James was dying. Books with the stamp, the tool itself, and the pictorial label using the same design, all remain in the museum today.

Fifty years later it was time for another impressive label to be engraved by Edward Ladell, printer of East Street in 1845. Two books support a third open to display a different view of the castle with space for the title and cost of the new addition to the collection. The society was last recorded in 1873; 959 volumes were passed into the care of the public library in 1920.

Golding of Colchester

Charles Golding was born in Bury St Edmunds in 1830 and married a Great Barton girl Elizabeth seven years his junior. Their daughters Florence and Bertha were born in London in the 1870s; at the time Charles dealt in books and manuscripts as Golding and Lawrence at 55 Great Russell Street. It was in 1873 that he moved the family to St Peter's parish in Colchester, opening his Ancient Literature Depot in Museum Street. The London partnership carried on without his permanent presence, at least until 1877. Sometime after 1894 he retired.

Despite never living there with his family, his heart was always in Suffolk and its history. He was ideally placed to collect Suffolk books, documents and coins and his published writing reflects his success. He was a member of the Suffolk Institute of Archaeology, the Kent Archaeological Society and the Royal Numismatical Society. In 1868 he published his *Coinage of Suffolk*, with illustrations of many of the pieces listed. In the preface he acknowledged the help of a wide circle of fellow collectors including Samuel Tymms, Ellis Wade, and Joseph Warren. His next major work was a detailed catalogue of seventeen *Scarce Suffolk Tracts* in his library, published between 1595 and 1684. Beginning in 1882 he supplied the *Suffolk Chronicle* with twenty-two numbers of an entertaining column entitled 'Old Suffolk, or Facts and Scraps, Notes and Traditions, of Local History'. The extent to which he drew on his own printed and manuscript sources is very evident.

His seal armorial bookplate (F12106) predates all his publications. The coat is that of the Suffolk Goldings, the three gold bezants almost canting. His motto is certainly apt: 'Sparsa coegi' – 'I have gathered what was scattered'. His illustrated advertisement for a local paper has much character and charm; of course the prices induce envy, but it is the rarity of several items which takes the breath away. The Landguard Pass Book, John Raw's Collections for Rishangles (with tomb tones!), Hawsted with 'not foxy plates', Almanacks published by various Ipswich printers between 1807 and 1826, and Hodskinson's Map of 1794 for only eight shillings and sixpence. For the Suffolk historian the Depot must have been a veritable Aladdin's cave.

CHARLES GOLDING,

ANCIENT LITERATURE DEPOT,

COLCHESTER, ESSEX.

SUFFOLK ARCHÆOLOGY. The Proceedings of the Institute of Suffolk Archæology and Natural History from its commencement, in 4 Volumes. (The first 2 volumes half-bound, the others in Nos.) Lowestoft, 1849 to 1873. Very scarce, good set. (The 1st Volume is so Exceedingly Scarce, that the Value of that Volume alone is nearly about half the cost of these). The 4 Volumes **4 4 0**

EAST ANGLIAN. The Original Set of the East Anglian Notes and Queries, in Four Volumes, from 1864 to 1871. Lowestoft (1st Volume half-bound, the remainder in Nos.) These are likewise excessively rare and scarce, when complete **3 13 6**

HAWSTED. History and Antiquities of Hawsted and Hardwick, in Suffolk. By Sir John Cullum. Best and Second Edition; good copy; not foxy plates, with good margins. Lond. 1813 **1 8 6**

BURY. Lady Monson, a Matrimonial Legend of Bury St. Edmund's. By T G Youngman. 4to, tinted paper. Bury, 1863. Very scarce. ... **12 0**

LANDGUARD. Patrol Book. Pass Words and Garrison Orders issued at Landguard Fort, for duty between the years 1761 and 1766. Numerous names and strength of Companies and their Fire Arms and Ammunition. By P. Thicknesse, Isaac Barre, George Coote, and others; with autograph signatures. AN UNIQUE QUARTO VOLUME OF 226 pages (Half-bound Morocco). These Works on Military Duties are most uncommon **3 3**

SUDBURY. Fulcher's Sudbury Journal, Nos. 1 to 11 for the year 1838. Local Intelligence, and long list of Birds found in the Neighbourhood, and List of Shells of the Locality of Sudbury. 4to. Now Scarce. 178 pages. 1838. **0 15 6**

WHATLOCK FAMILY. Will of George Whatlock, of Clare, and of his gifts to Clare Church. With notes. Bury, 1860. ... **2 6**

WITHERSFIELD. History of the Church of St. Mary at Withersfield, and of the Barnard and Jacob Families, and their Memorials. By S. Tymms. Bury, N.D. **2 6**

IPSWICH. Account of the Ipswich Wet Dock, and Embankment at Downham Reach, with a Diagram. By J. Hare. 8vo., 44 pages. (Scarce). Ipswich, 1836. ... **6 0**

COUNTY MAP. Fine large Map of the County of Suffolk, by Faden—Size 63 in. by 48—with plan of Ipswich and View of Abbey, Bury. Dated 1783. Mounted on Linen and in Case. Very Clean **0 5 6**

RISHANGLES. MS and other Collections Relating to Rishangles with Tomb tones, Inscriptions and Arms in MS. Also Portraits of the Grimston and Vernon Families, collected and formed by Mr. Raw, of Ipswich. In one Quarto Volume. 1826-9 ... ... **1 5 0**

COINAGE. History and List of all Regal Coins, Leaden Pieces, and Early and Local Tokens, with long notes on the Issuers and the Mints. By C. Golding. In one Quarto Volume with 70 Illustrations. Printed for private distribution only. London, 1868 ... ... **0 15 6**

HALESWORTH. Original Poems; Moral, Heroic and Pathetic. By a Traveller. Halesworth, Tippell, 1834. Contain the Halesworth Volunteers' Song at Lowestoft in 1804 ... **0 2 6**

SUFFOLK. Local Tables, issued with Almanacks containing all Local Names of M.P.'s, Justices, Bailiffs, &c., for Ipswich and other Suffolk Towns, for the years 1807, 1808, 1809, and 1810. By John Bransby, of Ipswich. The 4 numbers. **0 4 6**

SUFFOLK. Similar; for the years 1811, 13, 14, 15, 16, 17, 18, 19, 20, 21, 24. and 25, containing a host of Local Names and Information. By J. Steggall, of Ipswich. In all Twelve Numbers, 1811-1825 ... ... **0 7 6**

SUFFOLK. Similar; for the year 1812. By J. Bush, of Ipswich. 1812. ... ... **0 1 0**

SUFFOLK. Similar; for the year 1822. By J. Raw, of Ipswich. 1822. ... ... **0 1 0**

SUFFOLK. Similar; for the years 1823 and 1826. By E. Shalders, of St. Matthew's, Ipswich. The Two Numbers **2 0**

BILDESTON. Buds of Hope, and other Poetical Remains of Esther Pearson, a native of Bildeston, in Suffolk, 1817, with fine Wood Engravings, 8vo. London, 1855 ... ... **4 6**

OTHER LOCAL SUFFOLK WORKS

OFTEN ON SALE.

CHARLES GOLDING,

Local Book & Print Seller & Coin Dealer,

COLCHESTER, ESSEX.

Two Kingsmen, peerless bibliographical scholars

MONTAGUE RHODES JAMES (1862–1936), is almost a household name, mainly through his four published collections of supernatural tales, the first *Ghost Stories of an Antiquary*. He was scholar, don and provost of King's College, Cambridge, in 1918 going on to be provost of Eton College, King's traditional feeder school. His principal scholarly achievement was the calendaring of the medieval manuscripts in the libraries of universities, colleges, schools and houses countrywide. He also published masterly interpretations of such sculptural feasts as are to be enjoyed in places like the Lady Chapel at Ely Cathedral. There the iconoclasts had wrought their worst, but Monty could see what had been there.

MRJ was a shy bachelor for whom his studies were his life. His copious notes on the manuscripts in the Town Library of Ipswich which he dated 27 December 1893 show that he did not need a long Christmas vacation. He did, however, enjoy staying on the Suffolk coast where some of his most evocative stories are set. His simple but well-engraved armorial with single arms (compare the armorial for Mary Stewart Tollemache which Wyon engraved) is most uncommon and illustrated here with permission of the Fitzwilliam Museum where it is to be found in the V.M. Turnbull bookplate collection. Burke describes the arms and crest he used for James of Staffs and Salop.

ALAN NORMAN LATIMER MUNBY (1913–74), known as Tim, three letters from his third name, also wrote ghost stories and his collection *The Alabaster Hand* (1949) comes close to challenging the Jamesian canon. Munby's stories first appeared in *Touchstone*, the magazine of Oflag VIIB. He became librarian of King's in 1947 and wrote wonderfully readable essays on all subjects bibliophilic. He devoted nearly fifteen years to cataloguing the dispersed manuscripts of the 'vellomaniac' Sir Thomas Phillipps, Bart, of Thirlestaine House, Cheltenham. He also wrote his biography, because the baronet's absurd eccentricities fascinated him. His book label, like many other used at King's, has a line drawing of the famous chapel printed in orange behind the text. It would be good to know whether the two men ever met, as surely they did.

Montague Rhodes James.

A miscellany of labels

Some labels have been described elsewhere in this book, for example the large ones for Peckover and Hargrave printed in Norwich in about 1720.

What follows is a selection of the mainly unassuming labels made for East Anglian bibliophiles with more modest taste. It would be good, but impossible, to verify the subjective impression that in these eastern counties the ratio of labels to armorials and pictorials is higher than in other parts of the country. The survival of all types of ex-libris is a chancy business. After the dispersal of a large library of interesting works, most books marked with their owner's plate, there is a strong chance that it will be collected and recorded.

Again it is only an impression, but many of the labels illustrated here are decidedly uncommon; one might venture to suggest that some are unique survivors of what will have been a small edition or printing. Best of all, we travel from the owners of large estates to humble crafts-people; even a woodcarver's apprentice is represented.

Labels printed on coloured paper deserve careful examination, for some were hand coloured (therefore on one side only) after printing on white paper. Of the four examples shown on Plate III, two are printed on genuine coloured paper while those for H. LEACH of Wisbech 1817 and George Burrell are white on the reverse. Since Leach's is the only Wisbech label, it is appropriate to deal with it here. In the 1830 Pigot's Directory for Cambridgeshire, Mrs Ann Leach is at North Brink and Henry and John Leach are booksellers and stationers in High Street. This label is likely to be for the first of the latter. Could it be a larger than normal bookseller's ticket for insertion in books sold or newly bound?

Ladies labels

Some writers would be unable to resist the temptation to suggest that when married women first commissioned their own ex-libris, feminism was born. Women have surely always been entitled to mark their books as they wish, but just as collecting is said to be a male trait, there are many more men's labels than women's. Before the Married Women's Property Act of 1882, of course, a wife's chattels belonged to her husband. In the circumstances one could imagine some Victorian husbands taking exception to their wives' use of personal ex-libris. Circular and oval frames, not exclusively women's, were favoured.

In suggested chronological order:

*c.*1775 ELIZABETH KEPPEL (F17049)
In 1772, the Hon Elizabeth Southwell, daughter of Edward, Lord de Clifford, married William Charles Keppel, 4th Earl of Albemarle (1772–1849) of Elveden Hall. She bore him five sons and five daughters and died in 1817.

1794 Mrs SOPHIA UVEDALE, Ipswich, 1794 (F30202)
Sophia was born in 1733 to the Revd Samuel Uvedale, rector of Barking, Suffolk. She lived in St Matthew's parish, Ipswich where she died in 1819, and was buried at Barking. Sophia enjoyed cutting around the undulating typographic border of her label.

Mrs. SOPHIA UVEDALE,

IPSWICH,

1794.

1795 and 1810 CHARLOTTE PYTCHES (F24379 oval border and F24378 with palm festoon)

Charlotte was born in 1772 the daughter of John and Mary Pytches of Alderton and lived with her elder sister Elizabeth at Holbrook. She died there aged 92 and has a simple mural monument in the church. The more elaborate frame which appears to be etched was also used for a label (NIF) by James Corder of Great Coggeshall and Bury St Edmunds. Her version was printed in grey-green ink, but Corder's in black. Despite James being a good deal older than Charlotte (he lived 1756–1835) I suggest this was her second label.

*c.*1818 E.S. & H. LLOYD (NIF)

Elizabeth Savage and Harriet Lloyd were daughters of Richard Savage Lloyd, MP for Totnes, of Hintlesham Hall. He died in 1810 and when his son, heir and namesake died, eight years later, manor and hall passed to his sisters and co-heirs. The lozenge arms seem not to disqualify this ex-libris from label status. Neither girl married, and Elizabeth died in 1828 aged 71 and Harriet in 1837 aged 77.

*c.*1826 H[ARRIET] TURNER, Norwich (NIF)

Harriet, one of the clever daughters of Dawson Turner, banker, antiquary and botanist (1775–1858, see *ODNB*), was born in Great Yarmouth in 1806, and in 1830 married the Revd John Gunn the celebrated naturalist, vicar of Barton Turf and rector of Irstead (1801–90), and died at Irstead in 1869.

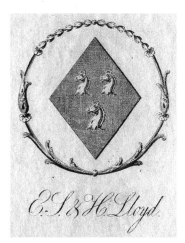

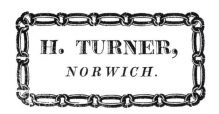

*c.*1850 MARY BURGIS. Stow-Bardolph (NIF)

Kelly's Directory of Norfolk for 1853 has Mrs Charles Burgis, farmer, from which we may surmise that Mary, widowed, had taken over from her late husband. This delicate label was pasted into a book published in the 1860s.

*c.*1895 JANE E[THEL] GATHORNE-HARDY (NIF)

Jane was born in 1872, one of the daughters of John Stewart, 2nd Earl of Cranbrook of Great Glemham Hall. In 1933 she lived at 9 Wilbraham Place, SW1. and died ten years later, unmarried.

*c.*1905 KATHARINE ALETHEA HAMBRO (NIF)

Katharine Alethea, née Scott, married Lt.Col. Harold Everard Hambro of Coldham Hall, Stanningfield, as his first wife in 1902. She died in 1938.

*c.*1925 MARY ROSE BIRD, Bradfield, Norfolk (NIF)

Mary Rose was another farmer's wife. Her husband William Bird farmed at Bradfield Hall, about two miles NNW of North Walsham.

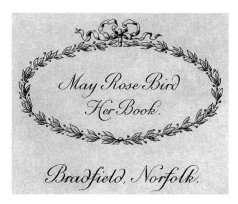

Five modest East Suffolk labels

The owners of these unassuming but highly individual labels were a farmer's son, a banker, a timber merchant, a surgeon and the proprietor of an academy. The only one whose profession and armorial crest is disclosed by the design is WILLIAM COLLINS WORTHINGTON FRCS. Born in Dover in 1800, he was already established as a surgeon in Lowestoft in 1823 according to Pigot's Directory. By 1855 he was in partnership with Daniel Meadows in High Street, but by 1874 his sons Francis Samuel (born 1837) and James Collins (1842) were his partners. William died before 1881 having been a widower for some years living at 41 London Road.

JOSEPH BERRY EDWARDS Esq., banker, features often in *The Southwold Diary of James Maggs*. He first married a Miss Elizabeth Bloom of Reydon in 1828 and was town bailiff the next year, senior partner in Onley, Harvey and Hudson's Bank. That July he was the senior member of a party on a fortnight's cruise to Holland aboard the *Providence* of Southwold. In 1842 he remarried Miss Ellin Meliora Hingeston, sister to Mrs S.B. Bloom, who bore him three daughters. He planned a change of scene for his new wife. After a dinner in his honour at the Crown (tickets 12s 6d) in 1844, they moved to Saxmundham where he ran the bank until his death in Bury St Edmunds, aged 60, in 1866.

JOSHUA FARRAR RANSON, son of Robert Gill Ranson and his second wife Elizabeth (née Farrar), was born on 25 March 1824 and entered Ipswich School as a foundation scholar in 1835. His parents were both paper manufacturers at Anglesey Mills in St Clement's, Ipswich. Father was one of the first aldermen of Ipswich after Municipal Reform in 1836, and Joshua became a councillor; both were liberals. For an act of bravery Joshua was awarded the Royal Humane Society's gold medal in 1844. He was at that time a wine merchant, but ten years later joined Brown and Co, timber merchants. Later, Ranson moved to Norwich, trading as Jecks and Ranson, timber, deal and slate merchants in St Faith's Lane, with branches in Yarmouth and Lowestoft. There he served on the city council, became sheriff in 1883 and lord mayor in 1888. Twice married, he died in May 1912 at Ingleby, Cotman Road, Thorpe Hamlet.

The owner of the label for F. DURHAM of Stratford St Andrew in 1844 is elusive. It is printed on magenta paper (see Plate III). Robert and Elizabeth Ann Durham (probably née Hunt, of Benhall) worked the 150-acre Pear Tree Farm there with four labourers, until Robert died aged 39 in 1845. In the 1851 census the widowed Elizabeth, still only 30 years of age, had a four year-old son Frederick. By 1855 she had moved to another farm in Little Glemham, in which parish, incidentally, Frederick had been born. No other Durham with the right initial has been traced.

ROBERT EVERETT was born at Leiston in September 1807 and married Elizabeth Marston at Aldeburgh in 1834. He does not appear in any Suffolk Directory except White's of 1844 when he was running his own Academy at Aldeburgh. In the 1851 census he was a widower, running a school in Calvert Street, in the Norwich parish of St George's, Colegate. His Stowupland-born mother Sarah, a 'landed proprietor' aged 70, was living with him, as was his cousin Emma Bobby, a farmer's daughter from Banham, of about his age. By 1864 he was retired, living at Mount Pleasant. It seems that his Leiston label was only useful in his youth.

Thetford labels

Though modest, the variety and originality of these typographic ex-libris gives them a certain charm, and none of them is found in Franks. Frame numbers refer to *William Davison's New Specimen of Cast-Metal Ornaments and Wood Types*, edited by Peter Isaac and published by the Printing Historical Society in 1990. Davison began his business in Alnwick, Northumberland, in 1780 and must have supplied provincial printers countrywide.

The earliest is WILLIAM ALTHAM's label printed about 1754 when he went up, aged 18, from Hitchin School to Trinity, Cambridge. He was the son of Peyton Altham of Latton, Essex, later of Mark Hall, to which he succeeded on the evidence of his later Chippendale (F429). Through some link with the Norfolk town, he became mayor of Thetford in 1784, and two years later was knighted. He died unmarried in London in 1816.

JAMES FISON was the founder of a great fertiliser empire, of which very little is now left. In 1830 he was a maltster in Bridge Street, but by 1845 he had diversified, apparently on the same site. He and his sons were now bone crushers and timber sawyers at their own Steam Mills. It was another Joseph Fison, presumably one of the sons, who by 1855 had established a larger operation in Ipswich.

GEORGE BURRELL's label on white paper, handcoloured blue, employs two elegant printer's devices (the upper, Davison 132) which are not confined by the broken rectangular surround (see Plate III). He was a son of James Burrell, ironfounder, and his wife Elizabeth Prick. He changed to a second label in black letter within a gothic frame, showing by the Latin 'Thetfordiensis' where he belonged.

JOHN BURRELL FAUX, presumably a connection of the last, was christened at St Cuthbert's in 1769, son of Gregory Faux and Bridget Burrell, who had been married at

William Altham,

Trin. Col. Camb.

JAMES FISON,

THETFORD.

No. *147*

G.B.Burrell.
Thetfordiensis.

J. B. FAUX,

THETFORD.

**Major Marsham,
New Place, Thetford.**

**Major Marsham,
The Rookery,
Thetford.**

**Henry Marsham,
Marsham,**

St Peter's in 1766. He was a grocer in 1830 but a banker by 1845. The frame of this label is Davison 909.

Major GEORGE AUGUSTUS MARSHAM was born in 1825 at Tours on the Loire, and inherited New Place in Raymond Street from an unmarried aunt Sophie. George, a bachelor, changed the name to The Rookery. The Revd Henry Philip Marsham, rector of Brampton, living at Marsham Hall, Aylsham, used an even more economical label. Robert Marsham Esq DL etc, father of George and Henry and patron of the Brampton living, lived at Aylsham Hall, Stratton Strawless, the family seat since the time of Edward I, and permitted himself the luxury of a stencilled crest plate. Later, George and Henry both moved on to die-stamped crest plates.

Labels elegant and impressive

CHRISTOPHER SELBY was born about 1675, son of Michael Selby of Castor, Northants, and was admitted a sizar at Pembroke Hall, in 1692. After ordination and proceeding MA in 1700, he remained at the college as fellow, bursar and eventually junior proctor until 1716. He could also hold the living at Grantchester nearby, but moved to a Huntingdonshire living in 1718, and to Framlingham with Saxtead as rector in 1728, where he died, aged 59 in 1734 as recorded on his floor slab in the church. His splendid engraved label (F26432) is hard to date, but it must be earlier than 1718, even by a decade or more, contemporary with early armorials.

RICHMOND GARNEYS (1698–1762), son of Clere Garneys, gent., after schooling at Beccles under Samuel Leedes, was admitted to Caius College in 1713, and entered Gray's Inn the same year. The family was descended from the Garneys of Spexhall, Ringshall and Kenton, all in Suffolk. Richmond was his paternal grandmother's maiden name. Two generations further back his grandmother was a Clere of Stokesby. He married Anne, daughter of William Churchman of Hillington, Norfolk, and their three children were Charles, Clere and Catherine. It is not clear why there are two versions [One is F11693, the other with the more rounded fleuron NIF], but the type is common to both. Even so, one fleuron of the wrong type has crept into each label. One might suggest a date around 1730 when the most popular square fleuron had gone out fashion.

ALEXANDER CLEEVE had a most delicate Chippendale label (F6043). Born the son of John Cleeve of St Margaret's Westminster in 1747, he went up from Westminster School to Corpus Christi, Cambridge as a sizar at the age of twenty. He was ordained in 1770 and became chaplain to the County Goal in Cambridge. He married Lois Lay at St Stephen's, Norwich in 1773, and died in 1805 at Knightsbridge. Venn describes him as 'one of the leaders in the movement for square caps'. It was in 1769 that undergraduates, who had formerly to wear round bonnets, petitioned the Duke of Grafton, about to be installed as the new chancellor of the University, to be allowed square caps so that they could attend the ceremony in a dress more decent and becoming. The Duke acceded to their request and the change was permanent. Cleeve also 'penned the ingenious though very severe tract *Somnium Academia'*.

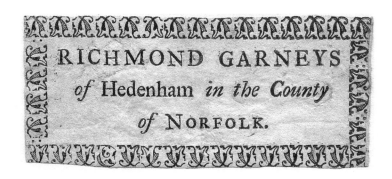

RICHMOND GARNEYS
of Hedenham *in the County*
of NORFOLK.

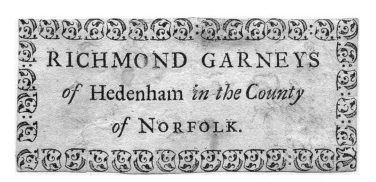

RICHMOND GARNEYS
of Hedenham *in the County*
of NORFOLK.

ROBERT FOULSHAM was in 1783 a silk throwsterer of Pockthorpe, Norwich, but by 1801 his widow was living at 32 St Stephen's Street. This very grand typographic label (F11100) indicates the profitability of Robert's craft.

GAWEN BALL, son of another of the name and Mary Goer his wife, was christened at St James's church, Bury St Edmunds on 20 May 1755.

WILLIAM RIX BLAKELY of Goswould Hall, Thrandeston, near Eye, son of William Blakely of St Stephen's, Ipswich and his wife Frances Rix (who probably brought her husband the Hall), was born in 1758 and died in 1781. This engraved label (NIF) is the only known example of the work of William Flindell, engraver and dissenter of Ipswich.

Three Norwich calligraphic labels

The Norwich Directory, published by William Chase in 1783, holds the key to these elegant calligraphic labels. Those of BARTLETT GURNEY, JOHN OXLEY and Mr IVES of Tombland have double oval borders in common, and Oxley's (and perhaps all three) could have been penned by Miss G. Gilbert who kept a Young Ladies Boarding School at No. 7 Pottergate-street. She only signs and dates Oxley's label (1775, NIF) for Gray to engrave (could this be Mrs Gray at No. 77 Pottergate-street?). C. Wilkin engraved Gurney's (F13089) and the Ives label (F16144) is unsigned.

From the *Directory* we learn that John Oxley was surgeon and apothecary at No. 28 Pitt Street, and Bartlett Gurney Esq. at No. 4, Red-well-plain. Mr Ives of Tombland presents more of a problem. Jeremiah Ives, jun. Esq. lived at No. 34 Tombland, but the Iveses who have memorials in St George's, Tombland are all John. One John died there in 1773 aged 43 and his son, born 1767, in 1824. In the absence of a first name, the identification of Mr Ives can be taken no further.

Six unusual Norwich labels

CHARLES TURNER, Esq., JP, born in Norwich in 1790, ran a boarding academy in Pottergate Street House but retired to The Crescent by 1851. His son and namesake (1811–1890) held Norfolk livings for fifty years, and was successively vicar of St Michael-at-Thorn and for thirty years from 1848 at St Peter, Mancroft. This elegant engraved label (F29974) is early enough to have been made for the first Charles Turner's father, so it may have remained useful for two more generations.

WILLIAM STARK (born 1788, F27941 overleaf) was a brother of the Norwich School landscape artist James Stark (1794–1859, see *ODNB*). William worked in their father Michael's dying business until the latter's death in 1831. An able chemist, he was one of the first dyers of fabrics of Norwich manufacture, 'particularly of the colour called Turkey red'. William was also involved in the Norwich art scene, lending pictures and serving on committees. A watercolour in the Castle Museum is inscribed 'William Stark aged 12 years *delt* under Mr Harwin's tuition, Norwich'. He was a fellow of the Geological Society, read papers to the Philosophical Society and was a director of the Norwich Equitable Fire Assurance Company in 1861. His sight declined in his later years, and for a few months before his death in November 1863 he was completely blind.

CHARLES SAMUEL HARCOURT and his wife Eliza Olley, both born in 1826 and married at 17 years of age, lived in Norfolk Street, Heigham in the 1850s, but he was a coach builder in Gildengate, St George's Colegate parish by 1881. His father Anthony was a heraldic painter and his brother Henry William a coach painter and builder. He was admitted a Freeman in 1847, and his son was of the same name and calling but of St Saviour's parish in 1879. The shield and its decorative surround is printed in gold with a space for a number. This label (NIF) looks like an ex-libris, but could also have been used by father or son to put the maker's name and number on a coach.

ALFRED KENT was 41 at the time of the 1851 census, living in Upper Goat Lane with a younger sister as housekeeper. His trade was shown as fowl merchant, but six years earlier he and his brother Thomas had been fishmongers in Upper Market. The label is printed on deep violet paper (Plate III).

In 1853, GEORGE EASTER was nineteen, the youngest of four children of William Easter, cabinet maker of Tooley Street in St Mary Coslany parish, Norwich, and his wife Ann. William was born at Swanton Morley in 1805. George was apprenticed as a woodcarver, probably to his father. In the 1881 census he was working at the Public Library and living in John Street, Heigham where his older sister Ann kept house for him. The label has the look of a wood-carving, and was probably of George's own devising, but whether designing it was a factor in moving him from his tools to his books we may never know.

JAMES LINCOLN was a very common name in 19th century Norwich. A tailor of that name was listed in 1823, 1830 and 1842 in St Augustine's. In 1854 there were father and son, fishmongers, in Upper Market, a baker at the Ten Bells Inn, an inspector of nuisances in New King Street and a collector of taxes in Lower King Street. There was a baker in King Street, St Ethelred's in 1860, also a brewer of table beer in Union Place. In the 1851 census the possible candidates were a silk weaver and hatter of 47, a fishmonger of 40 and a general shoe manufacturer of 38 years of age. It is anyone's guess which James owned this delicately engraved label.

Richard Daniel of Stokesby

RICHARD DANIEL was the second son of Knights Francis Daniel, Esq., at whose expense the National School at Stokesby was built in 1842. Richard entered Clare College, Cambridge as a pensioner in 1819 and was, by 1827, MA, FSA and a priest. After a curacy at Caistor-by-Yarmouth when he continued to live at his father's house in Stokesby, he held two livings from 1835 until his death in 1864: West Somerton in Norfolk and Combs in Suffolk where he was resident and a JP. His elder brother Thomas Robert owned and lived at Edgar House there, to which Richard's son eventually fell heir. Richard Daniel built the school at Combs in 1854, and 'much improved the bleak hill between the Ford and the Tannery' by building a row of model cottages, much admired at the time for their 'commodious-ness and neat appearance'. From 1854, he and his son shared the Rectory while Edgar House was let to a tenant.

Gibson of Saffron Walden

WYATT GEORGE GIBSON of Saffron Walden (1790–1862) was a Quaker and a banker whose book label had his name in bold black letter. By his wife Deborah Stacey he had a son GEORGE STACEY GIBSON (1818–83). For his unmarried sister MARY (1791–1839) he had a delightful circular presentation label made in black letter calligraphy in 1822. George, a botanist, married Elizabeth Tuke of Yarmouth, became FRS in 1847 and published his *Flora of Essex* in 1862. He used a label printed on greenish paper, but later and, unusually for a Quaker, an armorial with a motto meaning 'Open ye the heavenly gates'. None of these is in the Franks collection.

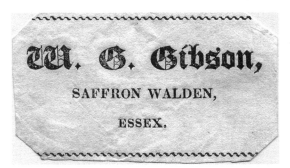

George Stacey Gibson.

Two medical men

JOHN NEWSON, surgeon of Woodbridge (1754–1829) was an early client of Isaac Johnson for drawings of 'Brood Mares from Stubbs' and voted for Bunbury (Yellow) in the 1790 County election.

JEAFFRESON MILES, son of another of the name and Dorothy Allen his wife, was a surgeon of Fakenham (1786–1844). He died at Knapton in north-east Norfolk.

Two corrections

SETH WILLIAM STEVENSON (*see ODNB*) chose the same frame as GEORGE PORRETT GRIMES, shown on the cover of *SNXL*, 2000. Unfortunately the frame was inverted on the Grimes plate compared with almost every other example of its use. W. Ticken of Norwich and R. Browne of Yarmouth used the frame as Stevenson did, bow uppermost. Only Grimes is wrong therefore; worse, no description was included in the earlier book. Briefly, George, son of John Grimes and Ann Porrett was christened at Stephen's church, Norwich on 26 February 1786. Thus he was only nine his label had the date 1795 added in ink. He is probably the George Grimes, saddler of St Stephen's Street listed in Pigot's Directory, 1823.

Modern ex-libris

The artists and owners featured here, sometimes one or the other, in some cases both, were or are East Anglian. They have been selected for the appeal and interest of the plates, few of which have been illustrated before. Some artists are included despite having made very few ex-libris. The plates and descriptions are arranged chronologically as far as possible.

JAMES REEVE (1833–1920) of Thorpe at Norwich (as the pictorial bookplate he lithographed for himself proclaims him) was, after fairly humble beginnings, the *de facto* founder of Norwich Museums. From 1853 he was curator of the collections in the building they shared with the Library and the School of Art. He assisted in the move to the Castle in 1894 before officially retiring but this left him more time for what had become his chief interest, the Norwich School artists. His own Cotman and Crome collection went to the British Museum, but his catalogue of the Norwich holdings was magisterial. He studied art himself and was a skilled lithographer as his bookplate shows. In the absence of a date we can assume this Art Nouveau design was conceived within a decade of 1900.

EX LIBRIS
HAROLD SHELLEY
SQUIRRELL

EX LIBRIS

LOLA BROOKE

ELLIS MARTIN (1881–1977) is chiefly known as the Ordnance Survey's map cover artist between the wars. He was effectively made redundant in November 1940 when austerity reigned. Ellis Martin and Augustus John were at the Slade School of Art together, but Martin's work was somewhat circumscribed and prosaic. His pipe-smoking hikers, bicyclists and drivers of drop-head coupés hesitate below fingerposts at crossroads to consult their maps before plunging into the idealised landscapes they survey. It was in about 1920 that he designed a pictorial, printed in brown ink, for HAROLD SHELLEY SQUIRRELL, born son of a corn merchant in Heigham, Norwich in 1873, but then the Catholic priest at St Benet's in Beccles. One senses the artist's enjoyment in drawing something quite out of the normal way of his work. Tanya Schmoller, widow of the typographer Hans, has it in a book of French poetry published in 1817.

CLAUGHTON PELLEW (1890–1966) was born in Cornwall, spent much of his childhood in Canada and studied at the Slade where he and Paul Nash became lifelong friends. In 1919 he married and settled at Gimingham in north Norfolk, where he seems deliberately to have sought retirement and obscurity. At the exhibition of his work in the Assembly House, Norwich in 1967 for which John Nash wrote the catalogue introduction, his pictorial bookplate for LOLA BROOKE was shown, signed and dated 1932. It is both bold and delicate in its partial symmetry.

GEORGE EDWARD KRUGER GRAY (1880–1943), made fewer than a dozen ex-libris (see Brian North Lee's *British Bookplates*, number 172). This stylish armorial is for HARRY LAWRENCE BRADFER-LAWRENCE (1887–1965), one of the pioneers of the Norfolk Record Society founded in 1930. He combined the offices of secretary and editor until 1935 when he moved to Yorkshire as chairman of a Bradford brewery. Bradfer-Lawrence, as a noted collector of books and manuscripts, was elected to the Roxburghe Club in 1934.

ANNA AIRY (1884–1964) of Playford near Ipswich was granddaughter of Sir Geoge Biddell Airy the Astronomer Royal. Her work in oil, watercolour, pen and ink, pastels and etching explains her elections as RI, ROI and RE. The modest and pleasing bookplate she signed for Sir HARRY COTTINGHAM NEWTON, Bt took John Collins of Maggs Bros. Ltd by surprise when he was cataloguing the library of that sometime MP for Harwich. A discreet crest and baronet's helm fills the lower left corner but the main feature of unpicked apples presumably alludes to Sir Isaac, from whom no one can claim direct descent. Sir Harry succeeded his father the 1st baronet in 1921 and died thirty years later. He was a noted yachtsman and an expert on Danish husbandry.

ANGELA LEMAIRE lives in the Scottish Borders town of Jedburgh, Roxburghshire. She has made fifteen ex-libris since the mid-1970s (see *BJ* 2006, page 131). This wood-engraved pictorial for the leading violinist FREDERICK GRINKE (1911–87, father of Paul the bookseller) who lived at Eye in Suffolk, must be an early one. It was to Grinke that Vaughan Williams dedicated his only violin sonata in 1954, because he so enjoyed the violinist's performance of 'The Lark Ascending'.

The Revd ANTHONY HOWE DENNEY probably adapted this seventeenth century library interior to serve as his own bookplate, adding his initials to the shield above and choosing a good Italic font for his name below. He was rector of Trimley St Martin near Felixstowe and a council member of the Suffolk Institute of Archaeology for whose *Proceedings* he wrote several important articles, also editing the papers of the *Sibton Abbey Estates 1325–1509* as the second volume of the Suffolk Records Society series in 1959.

Anthony Howe Denney, A.K.C., M.A.

MEG STEVENS provided ten wood engravings to illustrate the Aldeburgh Festival programme book in 1961 of which this one of Sudbourne church was a fine example. The other nine would still make excellent ex-libris. Meg and her husband lived in Colchester then where Roger worked for Benham and Company, printers to the Festival. The engravings could be printed from the wood in the days when Festival audiences were comparatively small.

The Revd G.H.K. Sherlock, rector of Sudbourne with Orford (the premiere of *Noyes Fludde* was given in Orford church in 1958), ordered the plate for his son DAVID SHERLOCK, a future editor of the Suffolk Institute of Archaeology's *Proceedings* and, much later, co-ordinating editor of the Suffolk Records Society. No doubt the bookplate was printed from the block.

In 1969 the Stevens moved to Powys where for Meg painting, particularly landscapes, took over from engraving.

Ex libris
David Sherlock

Sum Scarfei,
nec muto dominum

The pictorial and calligraphic labels of REYNOLDS STONE (1909–79), are some of the finest ever made. He made two for PETER PEARS and BENJAMIN BRITTEN, in 1968 a calligraphic label, and, two years later, the pictorial shown as the frontispiece with pears and lute. For the memorably kind and hospitable CLAVERING and EVELYN FISON at Stutton Hall the pictorial shown was commissioned in 1947. Sir Clavering Fison was chairman of the famous manufacturers for which Harvest House was the firm's headquarters towering above the beach at Felixstowe. The view of the Stour, photographed for Stone, is accessible by a path south of the Hall and the tree still recognisable.

Certainly not by Stone but an interesting typographic label for NORMAN SCARFE, historian, and author, *inter alia*, of Shell Guides and *The Suffolk Landscape*. Its short Latin motto is adapted from the inscription Erasmus used to protect his volumes from tardy returners. It was printed by W.S. Cowell Ltd of Ipswich in about 1960 when Norman was general editor and they were printers to the Suffolk Records Society.

ZELMA MACKENZIE (née BLAKELY) (1927–78) made wood engravings for book illustrations and bookplates. It is surprising that the Folio Society gave her only two commissions (Altamirano's *Zarco the Bandit* in 1957 and *The Charterhouse of Parma* by Stendhal twenty years later), for her work enhances both volumes enormously. For at least twenty years she and her husband Keith lived at Chelmondiston, and in 1961 she painted a lively and amusing barge mural over the bar of the Pin Mill Sailing Club.

She made over a dozen striking bookplates which Philip Beddingham listed in the Society's *Newsletter* Volume II, 164–65. Shown here is the Mackenzies' own KZ urn plate (Keith and Zelma) and for Diana and David Hunter (D & DH) a scene full of symbols, notably the huntress Diana and a warship in silhouette under a moonlit sky.

It was in 1981 that JOHN SUTCLIFFE made this pictorial armorial plate for BRYAN HALL of Banningham Old Rectory near Aylsham. Bryan and his father William Charles before him had many bookplates, some of no great artistic merit etched by E.E. Clarke. The Bonhams three-day sale at the Old Rectory in 2004 drew dealers and collectors from all over the country for pictures, silver, clocks and much else from that Aladdin's cave of antiques. Bryan died in 2005, aged 83. SHEILA ANN DAY, the cousin who kept house for him, had a pictorial armorial showing St Ives Bridge and the achievement granted to Edmond Daye in 1582. It was designed by ALAN BARLOW, renowned for memorable stage sets painted on strings and revealed by hoisting on long horizontal poles.

EILEEN CLARKE of Ipswich (b.1941), for long a member of the Society, has more than three dozen bookplates to her credit, mostly calligraphic pictorials cut in lino. For DENZIL REEVES, her tutor at Colchester School of Art, she cut Radha and Krishna and printed the block in blue on cream paper. GEORGE COOPER maintained a Wharfedale Press, and this strong image was printed for him from a zinc plate in black. JONATHAN WRIGHT, son of a friend and a Sir Galahad by nature, deserved his mounted knight in armour in black on white paper.

(90%)

(90%)

Ginny Broomhead

LINDA HOLMES of Walpole near Halesworth wood-engraves with distinction and many of her smaller pictorial blocks would make delightful ex-libris. The large plate for GINNY BROOMHEAD covers the owner's many interests in spinning, patchwork and gardening; the black cat merely looks on.

For the late CLAUDE and JOAN COX, of The White House, Kelsale, antiquarian booksellers in Silent Street, Ipswich until their retirement, the apple tree leans towards its rootlike shadow. The block was printed in 1997 by Sebastian Carter at his Rampant Lions Press.

ANDY ENGLISH, of Denver in Norfolk, lives at Little Downham, near Ely, and has wood-engraved a great many ex-libris for clients all over the world. One indeed, showing meercats under a night sky, is for our member Lewis Jaffé. Andy first engraved on wood in 1991, and likened the process to 'remembering rather than learning'. In 2006, aged 50, he retired from teaching to concentrate on engraving and printing, having built a new studio and restored an 1865 Albion printing press the year before.

His own plate for marking larger books is printed from two blocks, the lower one introducing his name. It shows at one and the same time his own sons, and him playing with his elder brother, who died tragically at the age of ten. He made Joan's plate showing their pets and the

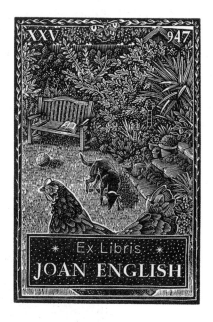

garden they had created together for their silver wedding (XXV) but the number 947 is a private message to her, which we need not puzzle over.

JAMES DODDS of Barnacle House, Wivenhoe has now made three bookplates, all pictorial. CHRISTOPHER and JULIET HAWKINS live and farm at Milden Hall near Lavenham, which presents an imposing Georgian elevation to the north. The Canham arms represent the family who owned the property in the eighteenth century, from whom Christopher is descended through his mother. The house was reduced from a linocut. DAVID YORKE-EDWARDS requested Stoke-by-Nayland church and its famous tower set in a lively land and skyscape for his bookplate, reduced from a scraper board image.

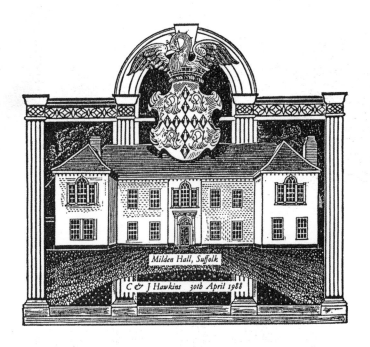

The foregoing were made in 1988 and 1990 respectively, but the recent design for BELINDA TRIM of Wivenhoe shows a naked tattooed and tousled woman sailing her boat through the waved pages of a book. The whole is splendidly conceived and brilliantly executed on lino. Sadly Belinda died, aged 34, in August 2006, having seen and liked her bookplate and just completed a first novel under her maiden name Belinda Starling. *The Journal of Dora Damage* was published by Bloomsbury in November 2007 to enthusiastic reviews.

Jamie's bookplates are all printed letterpress from zinc lineblocks.

JOHN CRAIG's bookplates were all but one shown in the *Journal* for September 2003. The author's great delight in the latest is his excuse for showing it first *and* last in this book. A few more than fifty immaculate pulls from the boxwood arrived on 9 August 2007, the very day Anthony Pincott received all the other images to be scanned for the book and began that labour which no author has the right to ask of any but a very good friend.

The initials jb and a stylised Suffolk latch (which also cleverly supplies the ly) conceal in a rebus the name and the county which both artist and recipient claim as home. In his accompanying letter John Craig expressed the hope that I would not feel it too big. 'My grandfather might [*did*] have something to say on that subject.' I replied that I thought it perfect in every way, truly believing that EGC himself would heartily approve.

Indexes

Tradecard or bookplate?